God is Enough

the alpha and omega of church

MATT BRAIN

ART BY ANDREW HOWE

God is Enough—the alpha and omega of church

First published in 2021
by Broughton Publishing Pty Ltd
32 Glenvale Crescent Mulgrave VIC 3170

Copyright © Bishop Matt Brain 2021

All rights reserved. No part of this publication may be reproduced, stored in a retrieval system or transmitted, in any form or by any means electronic, photocopying, recording or otherwise, without the prior written permission of the publisher.

Art copyright © Andrew Howe 2021

Typesetting by Sarah Crutch
Editing by Robyn O'Sullivan

ISBN 978-1-922441-03-4

Contents

Foreword	v
Artist's reflection	ix
Introduction	1

Part A: Being the church — 9

Chapter One	11
Chapter Two	29
Chapter Three	49
Chapter Four	65
Chapter Five	83

Part B: Ten reasons to be hopeful — 99

Reason One	101
Reason Two	105
Reason Three	108
Reason Four	111
Reason Five	114
Reason Six	118
Reason Seven	122
Reason Eight	126
Reason Nine	130
Reason Ten	134
Conclusion	138

Foreword

In this engrossing and stimulating book, Bishop Matt drills down to the core meaning of church and our part in it, both as individuals and as corporate members of the Body of Christ. He also shows how our God-given gifts, those innate skills and abilities, and those of the Holy Spirit become significant in good works, ministries and life of the church.

God is Enough helps us examine our present condition and look at new ways of using our resources to work for change, which can grow and sustain our faith and our congregations. It is stimulating. It draws us out of the torpor of habit and comfortable ritual, and even invites us to think about how we worship as church.

The excerpts from the letters of Paul are eloquently illuminated to give us great encouragement for our times. We live in an ever-changing world, as did people in Paul's era, dealing with competing demands of society and domestic life, as well as their effects on the many manifestations of church.

Bishop Matt focuses on five common pitfalls that congregations face in their daily working life, then gives us the great hope and encouragement of ten responses to counter those pitfalls, echoing the realities of parish life today. However, the responses make us think outside the usual box for solutions. The questions at the end of each chapter help us examine what we do, and how we do it, to form solutions.

As a member of a typical parish with an aging congregation and failing physical and financial resources, like many I tend to focus on what we don't have (an unhealthy and potentially terminal state) rather than concentrating on how to develop and employ the gifts of our congregation in order to build up what we have into what we want to have.

We are inspired to imagine 'What it would be like if...' Wish fulfilment for me is having a more youthful and vibrant congregation invigorating our present and future ministries. Bishop Matt encourages us to reach out rather than wait for people to come to us to grow our congregations. Certainly, this is do-able as most of us have connections in the community at large; just quietly and gently meeting with friends, and developing deeper connections, can lead to faith-based relationships.

There are truths that reassure and encourage us: that those who have stayed in the church, despite declining numbers and the legacy of scandals wrought by abuse, do so because of spiritual values and faith and therefore are highly engaged; that getting to know each other more deeply, and valuing individual special gifts, supports an understanding that disagreements with each other can happen while still remaining committed to one another and our common goals.

Bishop Matt tells us his stories: 'there are green shoots everywhere'. How exciting...that while there is decline there is also birth and rebirth and not necessarily in the old church mould. God's great plan for us remains the same, however the expressions of our faith are ever evolving. Today we think of COVID-19 as a destructive force for our church services – masks, shorter services, fewer hymns, restricted attendance and fellowship – but how inventive we've become with Zoom technology and social media. I can see us in my parish rethinking how we deliver prayer and praise. Out of the darkness of COVID-19 comes the light of connectedness and the determination not to forget our lonely and struggling brothers and sisters in Christ. I'm reminded that Jesus was upfront and personal with lepers and those seeking his help, and how easy it is for us to reach out today or stay connected and help one another simply by pressing a few buttons on a computer or smart phone.

Bishop Matt has given us much to contemplate; a living blueprint to sustain and grow faith and Church as we worship, work and live out our Christian mission in this challenging world, discovering that indeed God is enough.

Esther Waters
Anglican Parish of Maryborough/Avoca
September 2021

Artist's Reflection

Bishop Matt telephoned me to ask if I would be interested in producing a linocut print for the cover of his new book. I was thrilled and excited, then hesitant. This would be the first time my art had been truly placed into a public arena. I feared my work would be considered untalented and poor, not worthy to sit on a publication.

I met with Matt, and we chatted about his book, the intent of his words, and the working title. I nervously showed him some of my work and talked about the process I go through to produce a final print. By the end of the meeting, we had come up with an initial design: a rising sun with three radiating rays. Over the coming days this image would evolve to also include the Greek letters alpha and omega.

When carving a linoleum block, I sometimes find that there is a pivotal moment when what I set out to produce no longer exists in totality. There is a point of abandonment when I become lost in my art. I do not know when this moment will begin, I recognise it when it arrives, and I do not know how long it will last. There is an internal shift from the conscious concentration that strives for competence, where each cut is executed with fearful controlled intent not wanting to make a mistake. I understand this as my artwork existing in a restrained cognitive form, above all else it is the pursuit of technical correctness. Then something will trigger a shift, usually a small noise or a sweet smell. Conscious concentration recedes to the background, emotion replaces technical correctness, fear and control are abandoned. Each cut becomes pure joy, there are no mistakes. Time unknowingly slips away. I understand this as my artwork existing in a freedom affective form, I am knowingly in joyful relationship with God as I carve.

The cover image of this book features a linocut print that resulted from that internal shift. The linoleum block had been drawn up with measured correctness, each of the elements designed to be in precise relationship with each other. The outside frame and horizon were measured and ruled, the rising sun inscribed with a drawing-compass, and the rays angled with a template. I believe such ordered correctness is a result of my many years of naval service. My recruit-school instructor berated us with the quote 'a place for everything and everything in its place' as he cast his keen eye around our cabin during evening rounds (inspection).

My first cuts into the block were completed with painstaking slowness, I did not want to make a mistake and gouge out part of the horizon. My hand ached and shook as I gripped too hard on the cutting tool. Two New Holland Honeyeaters began to chirp in our garden, my hand relaxed as I listened to these birds share communication I would never understand. Joy flooded into my heart as I sensed the presence of God. The cuts into the block flowed with careless abandonment, it ceased to matter if the horizon was straight or the rising sun was perfectly arced, beauty or mistakes would be found in the eye of the beholder and no longer burden my hand. The first block took six hours to carve although at the time it felt more like thirty minutes.

I believe at times we all hold fear within us: an emotion that can be difficult to let go of. The prophet Isaiah – 'Strengthen the weak hands and make firm the feeble knees' (Isa 35:3 NRSV) – speaks to me and my fear of making mistakes. Fear in the heart affects the ability of hands to work for God and of feet to walk in His ways.[1] My fear of error had to be given to God and this was in-part accomplished with the aid of two small native birds. The linoleum block's technical correctness had been replaced with a naïve clumsiness that was carved with joy and abandonment, in relationship with God.

And so, a completed artwork, the elements of which demonstrate the effects of that relationship in the creative process, leading the beholder to consider the imagery and reflect on God...

> A rising sun, or maybe it is a setting sun? 'From the rising of the sun to it setting the name of the Lord is to be praised' (Ps 113:3 NRSV). The worship of the Lord is not tied to the start or end of the day, nor is it tied to a geographical location, it is truly universal.
>
> The Greek letters alpha and omega were carved into the sun to show that God is the absolute source of all creation and history; nothing lies outside of him; he is the one who has his hand on everything.[2] 'I am the Alpha and the Omega, says the Lord God, who is, and who was, and who is to come, the Almighty' (Rev 1:8 NRSV). In this linocut, alpha and omega have been printed from left to right, however they were carved into the linoleum block right to left. Many of the world's languages are written right to left, including Hebrew.
>
> Radiating from the sun are three main rays that represent the Trinity: the Father, the Son, and the Holy Spirit. Also radiating from the sun are minor slashes of red and black

---

1   G.W. Grogan, Isaiah, in *The Expositor's Bible Commentary Proverbs to Isaiah*, T. Longman & D. Garland (eds), Zondervan, Michigan, 2008, p. 696.

2   A. F. Johnson, Revelations, in *The Expositor's Bible Commentary Hebrews to Revelation*, T. Longman & D. Garland (eds), Zondervan, Michigan, 2008, p. 601.

indicating that the Trinity universally shines in all directions in the most unexpected manner.

The squareness of the red — which Matt saw as a 'stamp' — draws the eye towards the sun which may be construed as the opening of a tunnel or passage, the beginning of a journey to be travelled with God.

Andrew Howe

Introduction

Being part of the church is the most glorious calling. It is nothing less than collaborating with others on God's great plan to redeem creation. What higher calling can a person be given? Unlike the glamour that attends celebrity and royalty, the glorious calling of the church is worked out in each and every small and ordinary action. Charting meeting schedules, stacking chairs, vacuuming carpets, baking scones to share for morning tea, and gathering to discuss a book around the coffee table are all everyday activities, even if that book is Holy Scripture. Sharing life together as Christians is the story of one small, common activity after another because it is the story of life.

We know the glory of being caught up in God's plans and activity. We also know the drudgery and fractiousness of working with each other on the simple things that make communal life happen. However, we often forget where the two intersect. Where ordinary life meets the extraordinary, where the sacred meets the profane. Where the glory meets the dust.

As clergy, lay leaders and the whole people of God, we are called to share in God's life. Yet we are sent to do so in everyday routines. We can become overwhelmed by the majesty of our high call, making us susceptible to showy or misleading traps. We can also become disheartened by the sheer familiarity of church life. Yet, God is enough: we need no other assistance to avoid the pitfalls and take heart when discouraged. He is the alpha and omega of church life. The beginning and the end of our call.

Whether we lead or follow the path of others, we are each significant and irreplaceable amongst God's people.

I have had the privilege of working with God's people for many years. One of my unexpected blessings is that for much of this time I have been able to collaborate with whole congregations as they have sought to live out God's call together in their local environment. In sharing the worship and witness with these many communities of faith, it has struck me that the unacknowledged meeting point, between the Church's glorious call and the ordinary parts of congregational life, is where we are liable to fall into some common traps. In other words: in reaching for a version of magnificence, we miss where true beauty lays; or in desiring to be extraordinary, we miss the opportunity in the ordinary.

Our position in history, and the way that we have inherited our expressions of church, amplify the snares we are liable to fall for. Patterns of ministry are changing. These changes have crept up on us and have been driven by many things. Daily life has shifted as technology and contemporary forms of work and leisure impinge upon times that not too long ago were sacrosanct. The common acceptance of broadly Christian ways of thinking about the world has also altered. Where the church could once act as the central institution in society it is now pushed to the margins as an essentially private affair. As we respond to these changes there will be many occasions when our patterns of life and ministry need to change. This creates stress and the loss of beloved enterprises. Yet through all this there are some surprising opportunities for lively and joyous ministry to occur.

In facing up to various traps that can emerge in the intersection between the magnificence and modesty of our experience of being part of God's church, we are faced with a unique opportunity to choose what we do and do not do. How may we act wisely, judiciously choosing what is helpful and godly rather than simply slipping into business as usual? We can enact a pattern of life that is established on a firm foundation. Not with grand plans, but with ordinary activities that grasp hold of God's glory.

In reading this far you will have already noted a small dilemma in expression. I am writing to you as an individual about your relationship with the people you habitually meet week-by-week to worship God and exercise a corporate life together. I am also writing to you as an individual-in-community, so lurking around the edges you will also probably see that there is an even larger body which is part of the conversation. Each Christian is not a solo operator of faith. The connection with a congregation of others is a real, bodily relationship that is easy to understand. With these others we sing, pray, study the scriptures, share the sacraments, and seek to act out a public faith. It is also relatively easy to imagine an extended relationship with others who are not part of our congregation but share our faith, forms of worship and witness at this particular period of time. For some, the circle of those with whom they share this extended sense of fellowship may be through a diocesan or regional link. For others, the circle may be larger, encompassing links with people around the globe. As awareness of others grows, so the sense of connection and relationship is enhanced. This is a real relationship, even if the bodily link may be tenuous. However (and this is an amazing aspect of Christianity), our relationship with other Christians extends beyond our era, to encompass all those who trust in Jesus for life. Again, this link is a real relationship, although the ability to hear, touch and converse with these others cannot happen bodily. Yet.

Each of these relationships can be called 'church', even if the centre of gravity of each use is slightly different. I have preferred to use the term 'congregation' when talking about our local, habitual gatherings.

Although I may at times use church with a qualifier, like 'our', to show our immediate part in the larger whole. When talking about the others who share our faith in this, our era, I have tended to use the term 'the church'. As much of our relationship at this level is mediated through the institutions that make common life possible across different locations, in this book the words Parish or Diocese are most commonly used to describe the holding structures and common life of many local congregations acting together. Finally, I do write of 'the Church' or God's church. This is reserved for the whole of God's family whether here now, or as it has been throughout the ages.

I have found this small excerpt from the Rev'd Dr Charles Sherlock's book *Performing the Gospel*[3] to be a helpful summary of these different relationships; and which one controls the others.

> **A note on 'members'**
> 'Member' in older English referred to a limb or organ of the body (corpus in Latin)—an ear, eye, foot, heart, head etc.—as the King James Bible rendition of 1 Corinthians 12 shows. However, until recent centuries only a 'person' could act at law: a group could only have legal standing if classified as a person, a 'body corporate' or 'corporation'. Individuals who belong to the institution concerned are then its 'members'.
>
> When speaking today of the members of a congregation, it is this latter meaning that often predominates. The result is parishioners who treat church as a 'club' of people with a common religious interest, and clergy who see church as a corporation whose prime business is keeping its branches going so the local managers get paid.

---

3 C. Sherlock, *Performing the Gospel in liturgy and lifestyle*. Broughton Publishing: Mulgrave, Melbourne, 2017, p11.

Not so! In Christian use, 'member' refers to the distinctive part that each baptised person plays as organically linked to all the other members of the body of Christ. In this sense, I am not in the first place a member of St Georges' Trentham—I am first and foremost a member of *Christ*, expressing this (in part) through my participation in the life of that congregation.

God is Enough falls into two parts. Part A: Being the church, comprising chapters one to five, examines common pitfalls congregations face as they work through daily life together. These five chapters explore the ways difficulties can carry the seeds of growth. Too often we rush past obstacles and fail to discover the potential that is waiting to sprout. Part B: Ten reasons to be hopeful, which balances Part A, is a series of enthusiastic descriptions of why we may have hope as congregations, churches, and the Church. I hope that it helps to open the eyes of our hearts to what God is doing amongst us and our communities.

Part A: Being the church

The five great traps that we can fall into when ordering our lives as part of God's church are laid out so we can examine their respective causes and discover solutions to each. Too often we wait for the perfect resources to arrive before making practical movements to get going with what God has already given us. Similarly, we prefer to wait until new people actually arrive before making the sorts of changes that might encourage newcomers to feel welcome. In our high estimation of the role of corporate worship, we focus too much on what happens on Sunday morning and forget the other aspects of life over which Jesus has a claim. We also fall prey to the idea that if we find just the right hook to entice people to come and join us, they will then stay and grow as disciples. Or we are tripped up by the thought that if we put in a surge of effort now, our churches will get on an even keel and become self-replicating, meaning we can relax and enjoy the fruits of our labour. We mix up what we see of church and its enabling structures with the largely unseen work of the Kingdom of God. The wonderful news is that, common as they are, each trap is not fatal to our faith or our congregation. Rather, they may become the cause for us rediscovering confidence that God is the beginning and end of our endeavour.

Part B: Ten reasons to be hopeful

God is Enough would be incomplete if it did not progress to rejoicing in ten great reasons to be hopeful for the future. There are many more than ten reasons for hope, however there is a nice balance between the five great traps and twice as many causes for hope. Some of the reasons for hope are in God's character, or self-existent life, and what this means for us.

1. God is the God of the upside-down Kingdom, so it is exciting for us to be losing power and position.
2. We are people who pin our hopes on Jesus' resurrection from the dead…and his body still has not been produced.

Other reasons pick up what God seems to be doing, in spite of the position we appear to be in.

3. Despite our weakness and fallibility people keep on being transformed by God's power.
4. The seeming contraction of Christianity in the West is balanced by huge growth in the East.

5. Even if estranged from society at large, Christians who worship, live and pray together offer the best language for the marking of significant moments in individuals' lives.
6. Churches are one of (if not the only) functioning relationship hubs in Australian society.

Our hope can also grow because the nature of God's church means that we can offer our communities great gifts.

7. Local and global connectedness is in our DNA, and this is what our world craves.
8. In a nation where even banks and the post office cannot maintain a presence across the land churches have 'franchises' everywhere.

The final reasons relate to our continued existence in this era; in which sense the final words of the book are, 'for a time such as this' (I am harking back to Esther chapter 4).

9. Those of us who have chosen to stay are highly engaged.
10. While we might yearn for a national revival, there are green shoots of growth everywhere.

I have tried to write *God is Enough* somewhere between a personal reflection on the dangers and possibilities churches face today and an examination of the causes of church dysfunction or health. It is clearly a personal reflection in that I have not disclosed all the sources of my enquiry and frequently make assertions that should prompt you to say, 'Yes…but why?'. However, I step through each of these reflections in a disciplined way, following the pattern I wrote more extensively about in a previous book.[4] In each chapter of Part A, I explore the trap and why we may be tempted to act in certain ways. Following this we turn to a key moment in Scripture to discover where there are resonances with our experiences, and challenges to our assumptions. This discovery is then brought close to a key activity we share in Christian worship. The insights from our experience, scripture and the way we worship are then gathered together through a helpful theological insight. Finally, I suggest an activity or series of questions that may help us on the way to renovating our practice.

God is Enough could be used in different ways. It could simply be read privately, to fuel your thoughts and encourage a personal sense of satisfaction in God's purpose for you as part of the Church. You may choose to gather a few friends and read it together, discussing the questions at the end of the chapters over a coffee. Clergy or other ministers may use it to form a book club with their colleagues, to review how their call to be (in the words of the Anglican Ordinal) 'shepherds after the pattern of Christ the great shepherd of the sheep' is being enacted. Parish Councils (or other governing bodies) could work through the text over the course of a year. They could read a chapter ahead of each meeting, and discuss the questions and what implications they raise for their own congregations, prior to considering the business of the agenda. This is intended to be a flexible, useful book.

In this sense, *God is Enough* is something like a personal manifesto for the Church as we experience it day by day: its wonderful peaks and ordinary valleys. I hope this little offering may help you to glory in our God who has given us great things, and to take joy in our ordinary churches; for God is the alpha and omega, the beginning and end of all we are called to be.

---

4   M. Brain, *Wise: Transforming Pastoral Ministry*. Morningstar Publishing: Melbourne, 2019.

Part A

Being the church

CHAPTER ONE

Go with what you've got
(don't wait for what you wish for)

St Silas by the Overpass is full of wonderful people. There is Pal, who week in week out coaxes wheezing tunes out of the dilapidated organ. And Pam, whose tyrannical presence in the kitchen belies the delicious treats sent forth for morning tea. Paul the Greater. Yes, he of the larger-than-life presence and wild stories, most of which are true. Not to mention the Paul the Lesser, whose quiet presence always manages to cheer the weary soul.

As we look around, it is hard to shake the uncomfortable feeling that we are an unimpressive lot. We try hard and use what we have to the best of our abilities but are locked into old fashioned ways. It is difficult to see how great growth and change can occur. Our talents are meagre and resources thin. Oh, we have dreams. We see what other places seem to be doing. We read Jesus' call to 'Go into the world'. We passionately support missionaries doing brave things elsewhere. We even go deep into our savings to keep a ministry to school children happening in the local area. But our dreams seem to mock our capacity. It would almost be better to not dream at all!

Yet we do, and so we wait to be able to enact our plans to change and grow. We cannot grow yet. Not with our lot. Not with resources so thin. What would be the point of introducing a kid's talk…there are no kids! I would just get criticised for dumbing things down. It is hard enough to preach a decent sermon without jibs about windiness or pointed looks at the watch. The idea of a kids' club is just laughable. And now that we are talking about it, the lovely food that is provided for morning tea is made sour by the critical air with which it is served. How can I expect to run a newcomers' course, much less an event to welcome baptism families? They would be turned off immediately.

I will just wait for the right resources to come. Then we can begin to change, and maybe grow.

Great Trap 1: Waiting for just the right resources

For those of us who care passionately about the church, the resources we work with can seem slim and unimpressive. We struggle to pay the bills, so the idea of seeking out well-trained and skilled help is a faint dream, and the people we do have are compromised by any number of attitudinal or capacity problems. Given this reality, it is easy to succumb to a type of restless apathy. We are restless because we believe that growth is in our DNA. Jesus came to 'bring life, and life to the full'. Furthermore, we have invested so much of ourselves in serving the church because we know, deep in our hearts, it is through this awkward gathering that life and health and promise come. Yet the raw materials we must work with can be so dispiriting. It is exceedingly difficult to see how growth and change could come unless some new resources are injected from the outside. And so, we wait, marking time until just the right resources arrive.

Waiting can often be a good thing. We can eagerly expect the arrival of a friend. We can patiently anticipate the answer to a significant question. We can hope for the consummation of a dream. Yet waiting can also be a trap if it causes us to miss what is calling for our time, attention and care in the present. If lingering blinds us to the value of what we do have, and the cautious ways that we can grow that valuable gift, it has become a problem.

As we turn our minds to the reality of leadership within the church it is not difficult to find reasons why growth seems far off and unattainable in the present. Conversely it is easy to identify what we could do if we had better resources. Yet an approach to leading God's people, which waits for the right resources, strays into dangerous territory, reducing a precious gift to 'supplies to be expended' so that certain activities may be ticked off a list.

At its heart, waiting for the right resources before contemplating change or seeking to grow is insensitive to the people of God as they actually are, even if they are not as we may wish them to be. For example, a desire to find more money to import some talent to help us is another way of despising the people, whom God loves so deeply, as they are presented before our eyes.

So, if this is the trap, how do we proceed with what we have got, instead of waiting for what we wish for?

God's people, God's gifts

One of our most dearly loved, and frequently used, metaphors of the church is of a body. The body-metaphor sits in scripture alongside that of a bride, a building, a household, and even a family, fleshing out the abstract effects of Jesus' redemption of an amazingly diverse group of people.

There is something delightfully tangible and comprehensible about the use of a body to describe an entity that is both unified and diverse. It speaks to a sense of harmony and purpose while retaining the different aspects or functions that one or another part may play. What's more, it literally pictures the incorporation that occurs when God binds us to Jesus and each other.

Like our physical bodies the body-metaphor is both simple and complex. We experience our own bodies as a unified whole, yet are aware of each part and system as it exists. A runner will know the joyous flow of their whole being in flight while simultaneously paying close attention to the breath passing through their lungs or the drive from the leg propelling the body forward. Similarly, the body-metaphor is used to capture the way in which church is both the many and the whole. It encompasses all the congregations in all the nations throughout all time. Yet it also relishes the individual and sufficient part each congregation and individual plays. It helps us to discern the difference between completeness and sufficiency.

The body-metaphor is deployed six times in the New Testament to describe the effects of being incorporated into God's work. Depending on your view of who wrote the various letters in the New Testament, it was Paul – or at least a Pauline aspirant – who used this metaphor. The exact author of each letter containing the metaphor is not of primary importance for our purposes. What is important is that each use is in a letter written with a pastoral purpose in mind. In other words, the metaphor is deployed to help the existing group of Christians to grapple with the implications of their togetherness. As we seek to avoid the trap of waiting for just the right resources to come along, we will look at each use of the metaphor in turn.

Romans 12:4–5

For as in one body we have many members, and not all the members have the same function, so we, who are many, are one body in Christ, and individually we are members one of another.

Paul employs the image of the body to extend his vision for what the day-to-day activity of a Christian should look like. Paul is at pains to present for the Roman Christians, who he had yet to meet, the idea that living in the light of God's gracious mercy should transform daily activities. That is, their change in position in relation to God affects the mind, but then flows into action. Their actions would therefore become evidence of a different moulding hand.

Unlike the world around them, the recipients of Paul's letter were to see their own giftedness in a certain way. They were all given gifts. However, each individual did not hold or exhaust God's gift giving potential. Their gift was only part of what God had handed out. Furthermore, the gifts they did receive were given so that they may be used for the benefit of others. God's endowment to them were an act of grace designed to allow them the opportunity to share the benefit with others. Gifts they were given were not all the gifts which God would give, and even those they each received were not exhausted as being gifted in part and being graced for others.

By being incorporated into a body, the Romans were radically 'for each other'. Accordingly, their purpose was to be found in acting to 'fill up' what others lacked, their disposition was to accept that they would need to 'be filled' through the ministry of others, and their value was to be found in their relatedness with each other 'in Christ'.

It is significant for us to note that each of the Romans was to realise that they were indeed gifted, and that they were to revel in the exercise of those gifts. Yet their individual gifts were partial when compared to the needs of the whole body. The joy and confidence in being gifted was to be tempered by humility at the limitation. However, the humility was not abject or servile. Each individual was to find great purpose as their gift was expressed for the well-being and growth of the whole.

1 Corinthians 10:17

Because there is one bread, we who are many are one body, for we all partake of the one bread.

This passing reference to being a body arises from a common activity. Sharing the singular loaf in the Lord's Supper binds many individuals together in an indivisible, organic unity. Yet we can see that the common activity does not make the unity. This arises from the participation they all have in a single source of life: Christ who died, but lives.

Paul's use of the body-metaphor is embedded in a longer passage exploring the nature of freedom and idolatry. Paul seems to be underlining the distinction between license to pursue an individual's own ends with the sort of freedom that releases one from a bondage to self. In this sense, being part of a body allows each one to gleefully consider the other rather than be trapped in self-regard.

1 Corinthians 12:12–31

For just as the body is one and has many members, and all the members of the body, though many, are one body, so it is with Christ. For in the one Spirit we were all baptized into one body—Jews or Greeks, slaves or free—and we were all made to drink of one Spirit. Indeed, the body does not consist of one member but of many. If the foot would say, "Because I am not a hand, I do not belong to the body," that would not make it any less a part of the body. And if the ear would say, "Because I am not an eye, I do not belong to the body," that would not make it any less a part of the body. If the whole body were an eye, where would the hearing be? If the whole body were hearing, where would the sense of smell be? But as it is, God arranged the members in the body, each one of them, as he chose. If all were a single member, where would the body be? As it is, there are many members, yet one body. The eye cannot say to the hand, "I have no need of you," nor again the head to the feet, "I have no need of you." On the contrary, the members of the body that seem to be weaker are indispensable, and those members of the body that we think less honorable we clothe with greater honor, and our less respectable members are treated with greater respect; whereas our more respectable members do not need this. But God has so arranged the body, giving the greater honor to the inferior member, that there may be no dissension within the body, but the members may have the same care for one another. If one member suffers, all suffer together with it; if one member is honored, all rejoice together with it. Now you are the body of Christ and individually members of it. And God has appointed in the church first apostles, second prophets, third teachers; then deeds of power, then gifts of healing, forms of assistance, forms of leadership, various kinds of tongues. Are all apostles? Are all prophets? Are all teachers? Do all work miracles? Do all possess gifts of healing? Do all speak in tongues? Do all interpret? But strive for the greater gifts. And I will show you a still more excellent way.

This is the longest and most recognisable of the body-metaphor passages. It sits in an extended discussion about the way to discern how it is that the Holy Spirit is working and how an individual believer may perceive the Spirit's activity within themselves. Paul begins by pointing out the obvious. That is, a body is made up of many parts. He is at pains to point out how silly it would be for it to be otherwise, and then draws the conclusion that each different part is necessary for the body to be whole.

As Paul ponders the nature of a body, he seems to delight in pointing out a ridiculous situation. If bodies have parts, and each part is necessary for the whole, then the different parts cannot sneer at the others. This is so even if one is not quite sure what a part is for, or even if the part is embarrassing.

The final stage of the metaphor points out that the body belongs to Christ. The difference and distinction between each part is held in unity through their common association with Jesus Christ. It is the Body of Christ. That is, each part is given dignity and purpose through its association with Christ, and each part is circumscribed and kept in order through the same.

Importantly this use of the body as a metaphor for the people of God transitions directly into the 'love' chapter in which Paul lays out the 'most excellent way'. We must remember that for Paul, the pastor, his heart ached at the way the Corinthian church was operating, with people vying for power, recognition and control. He was not writing about love whilst in fits of transcendent rhapsody. Rather he was desperately sad that the Corinthians were not acting like a body in which each part collaborated in synchronous harmony.

EPHESIANS 4:12

> ...to equip the saints for the work of ministry, for building up the body of Christ...

Another of the passing references to the church as the Body of Christ is made in this Ephesians passage. At least two key points are made. First, that the head gives gifts to the members that make up the rest of the body. Gifts should not be read in a contemporary sense as being gifted or talented, but rather as presents arising from the beneficence of the giver. This means that being part of the body means to be showered with good things.

The second point being made is that in giving the artefacts of his grace Christ intends that the whole should benefit. It should grow into maturity. This extension of the metaphor is fitting. A body should grow and grow into its fullness. It is the distribution of gifts amongst the body that is instrumental in the growth. Some are given the capacity to equip others, yet it is also those thus equipped who are graced to serve so that the whole may thrive.

Ephesians 5:29–30

> For no one ever hates his own body, but he nourishes and tenderly cares for it, just as Christ does for the church, because we are members of his body.

The next occurrence of the body metaphor is found in the pastoral ramifications of revering Christ. Worshipping Christ brings the imperative of mutual submission. Amid a difficult and debated passage two further themes are drawn from being the body.

The first is that the church exists in relationship with Christ as its saviour. In this sense to be the head of the body is to be the enabling presence. The exercise of headship is less about power or control and more about generating life. This is why Christ 'cares for the church' and is bound as one with the church.

In this context, to submit means to receive the generative gifts of the giver, but then to act like the giver, bending all of one's power to that which will see others grow.

Colossians 1:24

I am now rejoicing in my sufferings for your sake, and in my flesh I am completing what is lacking in Christ's afflictions for the sake of his body, that is, the church.

The final passage amplifies once more that the church acts with Christ as a person's body does with itself. The two are indivisible. To be part of the church is to be joined to Christ, sharing Christ's fate yet imbued (all alike) with Christ's ever-living power. Interestingly, the pastor's suffering for the body takes on a Christological character, both in suffering as well as in life.

To be the body of Christ endows each part with incalculable worth. Indeed, being part of the body is something like being endowed with a certain giftedness. However, this giftedness is not discovered independently. Rather the giftedness of each part of the body occurs in relation to Christ and through Christ the others who make up the body. For Christ caused the incorporation of each one of us placing us in intimate relationship with each other.

A simpler way of expressing this is through the assertion that in being part of the body of Christ, God has gifted you along with those who are also members of that Body. The gifts may not be large or noticeable, yet they are gifts given by God. The part of the body that meets with you may not be a complete manifestation of the whole. Yet each part, when incorporated into the body, is gifted by God to perform service to the whole. Amazingly, this includes service to Christ the head, and the Father who has brought it all together. It is possible because the Spirit makes it so. Additionally, it means that each part – Pal, Pam, and both Paul the Greater and Lesser – are capable of acting in such a way that a watching world may be able to perceive the God who brought them all together with you.

The Lord be with you. and also with you

Recognising each other's true value is one of the challenges we face in contemporary life. The many ways that we talk about and interact with each other tend to drive us into a sorting of value and capacity. Sometimes this occurs explicitly as we look to the professional expertise or capacities one may claim when considering a person's use in a project. Other times it is more covert as we are drawn to displays of competence or a well-curated social media feed.

One of the magnificent correctives of well-wrought Christian worship is the understanding that we worship God with whomever turns up. Worship is an affair that engages each of us intensely as individuals yet is derived from a source that sits outside each one of us. It flows from a giver and returns amplified by the voices of many.

This is illustrated most simply through the episode of the Golden Calf found in the Book of Exodus. To worship the God of the Hebrews meant abandoning a best-guess mentality and paying attention to the God who disclosed a personal name. God was not content to have a people use a generic term for a deity, but drew close in the name of 'Yahweh'. Rather than building worship from the ground up through the production of an artefact that could then transmute the prayers and ministrations of a people into some divine good, the people of God were summoned to listen to the call of the one who was self-evident. Yahweh — I Am — set the ground for worship and in the call to come and acknowledge God's being, provided assurance that the people would find sufficient rest for their souls.

So, the demand to come to 'Yahweh — I Am' found its right conclusion when the people abandoned their best guess (a golden calf designed to look like the idols of those dwelling around them) and willingly bound themselves to God. The stunning thing about this movement is that the people who joined their voices to respond to the God who had given them intimate access were a mixed and motley crew. Their leaders had failed at key points and none of the whole had covered themselves in glory. Yet there they were. Full and sufficient at that time participating in God's purpose.

The greeting 'The Lord be with you' picks up this responsive two-step movement. The name of the one who calls out to a disparate and often inadequate people is invoked as I look you in the eye and assign God's value to you. Even more, I am delighted to hear you affirm, 'And also with you'. In this short phrase I am reminded that together we are called, together we come, and God is with us ready to will and to work in us, together.

Guidance and gifting

We have explored some of what it means to be drawn into the Body of Christ. We have also been reminded of the responsive two-step dance enacted in worship. Now it is time to draw our thoughts together. Accordingly, I have found it helpful to notice the relationship between God's gifting and God's guidance of the church which lies at the heart of missiology.

Donald Bosch helped to rekindle a deep and broad appreciation of the role of mission in the life of the church through his pivotal book *Transforming Mission: Paradigm Shifts in Theology of Mission*.[5] Bosch did not see mission as being a set of activities to be done tangentially, or coincidentally to the core work of being church. Rather, he saw mission as being essential to its very nature.[6] This idea flips our usual conversation surrounding Christian activity. We will often talk of sending out missionaries or supporting those who go out on mission. If mission is part of the church's DNA it exists as its constitution. This

---

5 D. J. Bosch, *Transforming Mission: Paradigm Shifts in Theology of Mission*. Maryknoll, New York: Orbis Books, 1991.

6 Ibid, 323.

means that the church does not only deploy some to be 'on mission' rather it is itself an artefact of a prior work. It is on a mission from God.

This understanding shifts certain activities from being the preserve of individuals to the whole Body working together. If mission is an activity of parts of the church, or individuals on behalf of the church, then it is natural that we would look for the most talented or capable exponents of whatever it is we are wishing to pass on or deliver. However, if mission as we experience it is the church being true to its call, or being what it is sent to do, then the various people and parts of the church suddenly and inescapably gain a role in this divine activity.

For the church to be an artefact of God's own work acts as a comfort to people who can feel they have little to offer. Even the least talented and most lowly share the same call as those most obviously capable of bearing witness to God's work in Jesus. Some of us feel this lack of capacity acutely and persistently. I suspect that all of us feel this at least some of the time. So, it is of great comfort to remember that responsibility for enacting a ministry which declares God's work to reconcile the world through Jesus is shared by the whole Body. Similarly, when we are tired and our hearts ache at bearing the effects of physical need and broken hearts it is a comfort to share the load with sisters and brothers similarly called to act as the whole body of Christ.

This very comfort should also be a spur to ward against lazy or fruitless ways. To be a people born of mission, and thus carried on in God's own work, means that we must be pilgrims. We are each alien and straining for home. It is too easy to be waylaid or side-tracked by matters that while not necessarily wrong do not add to the journey home in any meaningful way. To be a people of God's mission gives us the clear indication that God sets the parameters for our loves and passions. Accordingly, the Body of Christ is to be engaged with the disciplined process of stepping along the way ordained for us. Not ways of our own choosing.

It is not surprising that being a people formed and sent on a divine mission resonates with the 'body' metaphor we explored earlier. If the character of being church is informed by the interplay between the various parts of a body, which are enabled to have life and given direction by their head, then the call to walk step-by-step with God seems fitting. What is more difficult is understanding how this works in practise if the parts of the body one is working with seem dull or poorly suited to any sort of activity.

Just do it!

As a young athlete I had a fantastic poster of the then world record holder for the men's 400m. He was surging up a hill flanked by the then unusual sight of wind turbines. The poster was advertising a certain brand of shoes, and the slogan was 'Just Do It!' I was no world champion, I did not even own a pair of those shoes, but the image did spur me on to get out and run. I could not wait until I could afford the shoes, or magically got faster, I had to just get out there and run!

Waiting for just the right resources before beginning the work we are called to do has two consequences. Waiting for something to happen without doing anything dooms one's hopes to failure. Even more importantly it will make us blind to God's charism and guidance. Logic will tell us that waiting for an outside input before acting differently places us at the mercy of actions which may never occur and actors who may never arrive. In other words, waiting very quickly turns into stasis, which in turn makes us stale. Just as a by-water will become airless and dead, full of algae and weed but nothing much else, so a church that does not begin to act in the ways it believes it is called will become choked and snarled. As a church waits for others to arrive (or, even worse, more money to arrive so it can pay someone else) before cautiously having a go at what God has called it to do. It grows stagnant and slowly insensitive to that very call.

We have seen that God does, in fact, give gifts to his people; each and every one. We have also seen that in drawing us to himself God simultaneously gathers us in and sends us out. The amazing thing is that this is true for the church as it is, not simply for the church as we wish it might be. To wait before acting in concert with God's call indicates that we have become blind to the real people with real gifts who share the Body of Christ with us here and now. In becoming blind to the way God has gifted each other, we then become blind to the places God is calling us to go. Conversely, acting in ways that reflect God's empowering gifts and with what God has given us opens surprising opportunities.

As we pay attention to the Body of Christ as it exists around us, we will have the privilege of discovering that God has gifted it extraordinarily. Too often when planning our ministries, or deciding what we should focus our energies upon, we try to plan what should occur before we look carefully at each other to ask what good works God has prepared in advance for us to be doing. Yet when time is taken to discover the different ways God has equipped and enabled each part of the Body of Christ, ways for every member to take up their part emerge. The energy required to 'just do it' in gathering people, as they are, to collaborate on God's call for our part of the church, may well be high. But it is a joy to discover how and where surprising people grow into their God-given capacities. The shape of what we wish, and have been waiting, for may be different, but the fruit that God brings is no less significant.

There are also great benefits for those called to lead the church in its life and witness. The minister is freed to act as a sort of 'spiritual archaeologist' whose task, and delight, is dusting off the gifts that

God has given the Body. Just as an archaeologist will patiently and carefully brush away the dust of millennia to expose a treasure beneath, those who lead the church are freed to help all who form the Body of Christ be free of the accretions which hinder that which God has given them. Rather than being confined to teaching or administrating or convening the Christian leader is given the opportunity to uncover that which God has already given. No longer is the minister a Sisyphusian character doomed to be rolling a boulder up a steep hill. Rather they become the enabler of those around them. In biblical language, they can shepherd the people for whom they care. The shepherd delighting in the growth they see and are at pains to seek out ways that each person may become more adept in what God has made them to be.

The people we meet with and the churches we form are a mixture of insufficiency and capacity. Insufficient because they are made up of people who cannot do all things and are beset with all sorts of frailty. Greatly capable because they have been called together by a God who loves them dearly and has decided to use them in his world-changing plans.

So, whilst we seek to go with what we have got, rather than waiting for what we wish for, here are three questions to ask as we become spiritual archaeologists for each other:

1

I wonder why God has made [insert name here] to be so passionate about [insert their passion here]?

2

What is this concern telling me about the needs for our world we can be serving?

3

What would [insert name here] need to be able to grow in their capacity to serve this need?

Just do it!

CHAPTER TWO

Behave like you want to become

I have never met an unwelcoming church. Or to put it another way, every church I have worked with is 'welcoming'. Pal, Pam and the Greater and Lesser Pauls are adamant that welcoming is in their DNA. Indeed, anyone who walks through the door will find a home with them. And that is true, from their perspective. All the same I do find myself smiling wryly that, even endowed with a position of trust and a visible 'place' within the church, I find that not infrequently I have to make the first move to relate when I visit. Around the urn at the end of the service we all muse at the lack of young families in church these days. When I gently suggest to Pal that he might like to learn a child-friendly song to lead us in, his reply is that he will…when kids turn up. Or when I muse that it would be difficult for the parents to restrain their children's appetite when the morning tea treats are brought out, Pam bluntly states that if only parents these days taught their kids to behave there would be no problem.

One of the complications of being human is our hard-wired desire for comfort and comfortable ways. Often this propensity will rear its head when we excuse behaviours that fly in the face of the very values we hold. Comfort and comfortable ways will cause us to become insular and conservative, preferring to maintain our habitual way of doing things even if it hinders growth. Necessary, even longed for, change is a future demand. One that we will meet when the time is right.

Before we all sneer at this attitude, I must admit that it makes perfect sense. Why should we contemplate change from a comfortable, serviceable routine? When so much of life demands energy and risk there is much to be said for dependability and the opportunity to rest. Furthermore, why act in ways that seem (at face value) unnatural or contrary to the norm? Especially if the norm has served us well.

Pal, Pam and the two Pauls are no different from any of us as they approach matters of change. Without the direct stimulus of need demanding attention, we will tend to remain content with familiar ways. These familiar ways may not even be old-fashioned, but they are a comfortable rut. We may not have any objection to change. We may even desire a change because we can see that change can often stimulate growth within us and the church. Yet the prompt to kick-start that movement? Well that can be tricky.

Great Trap 2: We'll change when new people come

Churches are unique institutions in that their activities exist as reasons to be rather than ends in themselves. Football clubs exist to play football. Bridge clubs exist to play bridge. Banks exist to store and transact money. Governments exist to regulate behaviour. But churches exist to shape people into the likeness of Christ. Our activities matter, but they matter because they ultimately either help or hinder us in being formed into the people God wants us to be. Our activities are instrumental rather than being ends in themselves (terminal). They are purposeful but the end to which they contribute (mightily) sits outside of them.

Our unique calling amplifies the difficulty in facing up to change. A bank may force changed lending practices upon itself because its capacity to transact money will be taken away if it does not. A bridge club may fold if there are not enough members able to play a game. Churches do not have this luxury, because as we were reminded earlier, together they form the body of Christ. As we contemplate change, *what* we are doing inevitably turns to *why* we are doing it and then *how* this shapes me and my inner life. There is an apparent logic in waiting to change until new people come. Why do something demanding and uncomfortable before it is necessary? Yet there are spiritual and pragmatic traps in choosing to wait.

Much like a prevailing current, comfort has a certain spiritual pull. But unlike a current pulling a vessel downstream, comfort will tend toward eddies that eventually fade into stagnation. Spiritually the effect of this stagnation plays out in a certain kind of selfishness. Usually this is not the sort of naked and aggressive selfishness that may prompt us to roll the eyes and cry 'grow up!'. Rather it is a more benign and passive kind of apathy towards other people. I might not have any problem with you and what you need, but the effort of preparing to meet you in them defeats me.

Pragmatically the hidden trap in waiting until others arrive before changing is that it is self-defeating. In an entity that is focussed on people *being* the body of Christ, the way we are towards others will usually play a determinative role in their willingness to join in and *be* the body too.

These spiritual and pragmatic traps are not surprising when we remember that we are part of an embodied, incarnate world. In other words, what we do and who we are cannot be readily separated. The actions we perform, or behaviours we manifest, have a deep and abiding impact on the persons we are. This is not only true for us as individuals, but also for us as individuals seeking to relate to others. If the possibility of changed behaviour is cut off until it is demanded of us, we will discover that we have been formed in attenuated and diminished ways. If our actions only ever follow our self-interest, we will be self-interested people. The reverse is also true. If we are prepared to try out some changed behaviours before they are actually necessary, our being – both individual and the manifestation of Christ's body – is more likely to be open to the unique demands of those whom God is preparing to join us.

The gifts of the spirit

As we explored the metaphor of the body, we already considered something of what makes the Corinthian letters a helpful primer in church life. But we will go back again to 1 Corinthians to take a closer look at the chapters in which the longest of the 'body' passages sits. I have found this to be a helpful starting point to think about change because of its overt theme, being gifted by God, and because of the hidden way that Paul writes to a pastoral context.

The short version of the deep pastoral relationship Paul had with the Corinthian Christians is that it was tricky and difficult! It was tricky because, like us, Paul and the Corinthians came to the Christian life with backstories. Additionally, these backstories shaped and coloured the way that they understood the world around them, and their roles and values in that world. In reading the chapters leading up to Chapter 12, which is our key passage, we can see that Paul is at pains to address the different ways that the Corinthians had become accustomed to relating to each other. It seems that a sort of spiritual brashness and verbal aggression was not only tolerated but praised. Negotiating these hard-wired patterns of behaviour was not easy. It follows that being part of a continuing and nurturing pastoral relationship was difficult. This is exactly what we hear from Paul, and this is where we can begin to think about change. Change is usually tricky…and often difficult. Therefore, it will take time, patience and the application of God's gifts if it is to occur.

WHERE IS OUR FOCUS?
1 CORINTHIANS CHAPTER 11

Now in the following instructions I do not commend you, because when you come together it is not for the better but for the worse. For, to begin with, when you come together as a church, I hear that there are divisions among you; and to some extent I believe it. Indeed, there have to be factions among you, for only so will it become clear who among you are genuine. When you come together, it is not really to eat the Lord's supper. For when the time comes to eat, each of you goes ahead with your own supper, and one goes hungry and another becomes drunk. What! Do you not have homes to eat and drink in? Or do you show contempt for the church of God and humiliate those who have nothing? What should I say to you? Should I commend you? In this matter I do not commend you! For I received from the Lord what I also handed on to you, that the Lord Jesus on the night when he was betrayed took a loaf of bread, and when he had given thanks, he broke it and said, "This is my body that is for you. Do this in remembrance of me." In the same way he took the cup also, after supper, saying, "This cup is the new covenant in my blood. Do this, as often as you drink it, in remembrance of me." For as often as you eat this bread and drink the cup, you proclaim the Lord's death until he comes. Whoever, therefore, eats the bread or drinks the cup of the Lord in an unworthy manner will be answerable for the body and blood of the Lord. Examine yourselves, and only then eat of the bread and drink of the cup. For all who eat and drink without discerning the body, eat and drink judgment against themselves. For this reason many of you are weak and ill, and some have died. But if we judged ourselves, we would not be judged. But when we are judged by the Lord, we are disciplined so that we may not be condemned along with the world. So then, my brothers and sisters, when you come together to eat, wait for one another. If you are hungry, eat at home, so that when you come together, it will not be for your condemnation. About the other things I will give instructions when I come.

Chapter 11 concludes with some of the words that I find hardest to read in the whole Bible. Verse 33 reads, '...when you come together to eat, wait for one another'. In ten words Paul exposes a culture that is turning the high point of worship (the Lord's Supper) into a competition for priority. Images of the scrum around the fairy bread at a child's birthday party come to mind. The largest or most forceful of guests pushing over the smaller or more timid. The reason I find this verse hard to read is that it speaks to a disposition that utterly misses the glory of what God has given us, and in doing so spoils this gift for those who seem to be weak.

My heart soars as I read Paul rehearsing Jesus' own words which we have taken into prayers of thanksgiving. I am drawn to savour the depth of Jesus' sacrifice and God's continuing provision of life. Paul's assessment, that the Corinthians do not discern 'the body' as they push and pull and contend with each other causes me pain. How can their focus descend so quickly from Christ to self? I suspect the answer lays in those sad words, 'wait for one another'. If our focus is on ourselves rather than each other, we supplant God's gift, and turn grace into mere fodder.

WHAT IS OUR GOAL?
1 CORINTHIANS CHAPTER 12

Now concerning spiritual gifts, brothers and sisters, I do not want you to be uninformed. You know that when you were pagans, you were enticed and led astray to idols that could not speak. Therefore I want you to understand that no one speaking by the Spirit of God ever says "Let Jesus be cursed!" and no one can say "Jesus is Lord" except by the Holy Spirit. Now there are varieties of gifts, but the same Spirit; and there are varieties of services, but the same Lord; and there are varieties of activities, but it is the same God who activates all of them in everyone. To each is given the manifestation of the Spirit for the common good. To one is given through the Spirit the utterance of wisdom, and to another the utterance of knowledge according to the same Spirit, to another faith by the same Spirit, to another gifts of healing by the one Spirit, to another the working of miracles, to another prophecy, to another the discernment of spirits, to another various kinds of tongues, to another the interpretation of tongues. All these are activated by one and the same Spirit, who allots to each one individually just as the Spirit chooses. For just as the body is one and has many members, and all the members of the body, though many, are one body, so it is with Christ. For in the one Spirit we were all baptized into one body—Jews or Greeks, slaves or free—and we were all made to drink of one Spirit. Indeed, the body does not consist of one member but of many. If the foot would say, "Because I am not a hand, I do not belong to the body," that would not make it any less a part of the body. And if the ear would say, "Because I am not an eye, I do not belong to the body," that would not make it any less a part of the body. If the whole body were an eye, where would the hearing be? If the whole body were hearing, where would the sense of smell be? But as it is, God arranged the members in the body, each one of them, as he chose. If all were a single member, where would the body be? As it is, there are many members, yet one body. The eye cannot say to the hand, "I have no need of you," nor again the head to the feet, "I have no need of you." On the contrary, the members of the body that seem to be weaker are indispensable, and those members of the body that we think less honorable we clothe with greater honor, and our less respectable members are treated with greater respect; whereas our more respectable members do not need this. But God has so arranged the body, giving the greater honor to the inferior member, that there may be no dissension within the body, but the members may have the same care for one another. If one member suffers, all suffer together with it; if one member is honored, all rejoice together with it. Now you are the body of Christ and individually members of it. And God has appointed in the church first apostles, second prophets, third teachers; then deeds of power, then gifts of healing, forms of assistance, forms of leadership, various kinds of tongues. Are all apostles? Are all prophets? Are all teachers? Do all work miracles? Do all possess gifts of healing? Do all speak in tongues? Do all interpret? But strive for the greater gifts. And I will show you a still more excellent way.

My sadness at the end of Chapter 11 then breaks. Paul commences Chapter 12 rather sternly, but a glorious reality pierces the clouds like the first ray after a storm. The Corinthians are gifted by God; motley, unlovely and rough group that they are. Once they were gifted by God, but now they are. What is more, they are gifted at the same time as Paul is chiding them for pushing and shoving around the Lord's table. This speaks to me of God's great triumph over our weakness. God gives gifts through the Spirit, and can do so even in the midst of our frailty.

And these gifts from God will pull our focus away from ourselves. The gifts of God's Spirit have the same origin, the same master and the same goal, even as they are performed differently by different people. In other words, the gifts may take a variety of manifestations, but they each have the same goal. This is why the metaphor is so apt.

And the goal? The purpose? The intent? That everyone benefits!

HOW WILL WE KNOW WE ARE DOING WELL?
1 CORINTHIANS CHAPTER 13

If I speak in the tongues of mortals and of angels, but do not have love, I am a noisy gong or a clanging cymbal. And if I have prophetic powers, and understand all mysteries and all knowledge, and if I have all faith, so as to remove mountains, but do not have love, I am nothing. If I give away all my possessions, and if I hand over my body so that I may boast, but do not have love, I gain nothing. Love is patient; love is kind; love is not envious or boastful or arrogant or rude. It does not insist on its own way; it is not irritable or resentful; it does not rejoice in wrongdoing, but rejoices in the truth. It bears all things, believes all things, hopes all things, endures all things. Love never ends. But as for prophecies, they will come to an end; as for tongues, they will cease; as for knowledge, it will come to an end. For we know only in part, and we prophesy only in part; but when the complete comes, the partial will come to an end. When I was a child, I spoke like a child, I thought like a child, I reasoned like a child; when I became an adult, I put an end to childish ways. For now we see in a mirror, dimly, but then we will see face to face. Now I know only in part; then I will know fully, even as I have been fully known. And now faith, hope, and love abide, these three; and the greatest of these is love.

Accordingly, we arrive at 1 Corinthians 13. This is the chapter read at so many weddings for its poetic description of what love is (and what it is not). Yet, this 'wedding chapter' is not about romantic love at all. Rather, it is Paul's paean to ordinary church life. Resounding gongs and clanging cymbals portray each of us as we push and pull with elbows out to establish our own place within the body of Christ. The very act of operating as if we must establish ourselves, not only diminishes but actually sours the unified body that Jesus has established.

So how can we know if we are doing well? What is the test to apply to ensure that the whole body is growing? Paul answers this in two ways. The first is Chapter 13 itself, in all its poetic beauty. We know we are doing well when love reigns, because love is the tangible artefact of the gifts operating each for the other. Being patient, kind, not envious or boastful, nor arrogant or rude, and so on (see verses 4–7) are the practical expression of love. Showing these internal characteristics is evidence that we are living in love.

The second test arrives in Chapter 14 and speaks directly to a very 'Corinthian' issue. One of the ways that the Corinthian Christians had brought the world they grew up in, and assumed to be normal, into the church was to see the most expressive and obvious spiritual gifts as being the most valuable. This was because these gifts could be perceived as lending divine competence to a person. It was the spiritual equivalent of being a fine speaker or successful businessperson. However, Paul subverts the outward showiness of the gift and asks about the outcome. In other words, he enquires as to whether the gift will edify or build up someone else. Paul muses on the question, "will folk be able to say 'Amen' with me after I finish speaking?". At the end of the day, the key imperative for the spiritually gifted person is how they can help someone else 'live into' what God has expressed through the gift.

Leaving and returning

We glimpse in the Corinthian letters the trap of local church life even as we see the possibilities given by the way God gifts us. It is all too easy for us to become insular and self-serving, though it would no doubt revolt us to discover we had become so. The nature of a community called together by God is that we look outwards and seek for others to be built up and encouraged. This is the purpose for which God's gifts are designed.

The Corinthian tension is the tension of the ordinary Christian life. In many ways it is a consequence of the dual locations of the church: a cloister where individuals are shut away, protected from the hurly-burly and given peace and calm to be nurtured; or a marketplace where one is always looking out to ask how to interact with those around.

Our own patterns of worship give us a helpful way to balance this tension. Which is not surprising, given that our form is derived from Jesus' example. It would be difficult to sustain a view that Jesus was not intensely involved in everyday life. The Gospels show him continually navigating other people's demands with astounding grace and care. However, we also see Jesus turn aside to be refreshed by God and, in so doing, be able to return and engage once more. Our pattern of well-formed worship is the same as that of Jesus: to consciously turn aside from the marketplace, and then to be sent out to engage once more.

A well-designed act of corporate worship withdraws from daily life and enters into a time devoted to God. It will progress through hearing from God and digesting what God has to say, to responding and being refreshed and enlivened by God's Spirit. It concludes as the refreshed body of Christ renews its call to be God's witnesses and is sent back out into the world.

Entering in

Irrespective of the location, good worship will cause people to step over a threshold. The physical layout of a space may help, but the call to summon God's people to be together in a corporate act, in which we seek out God's guidance and sustenance, is a threshold of the heart. Traditionally, the summons 'The Lord be with you' is not a marker of time or even a *de facto* alarm. Rather it is the focussed cry of the people gathered to do business with God and is returned by the whole with the corporate 'And also with you!'.

The songs and prayers that follow should frame this movement – from the outside with the world to the quiet space inside with God. It is our movement with Jesus to the quiet place in which our hearts are given an exclusive space to yearn after God.

Hearing and digesting

Having withdrawn with Jesus, across the threshold of the heart, it is appropriate to seek out God's living word. An amazing and distinctive aspect of the Christian faith is the expectation that God has and will continue to communicate with his people. As those hearing God's voice we do not come in dryness and a sense of compliant resignation, but with the expectation that treasures old and new will be uncovered.

Our first step is to withdraw over a threshold of the heart but now find ourselves in a new dwelling with a number of rooms. So, engaging with scripture by means of reading, praying, and singing, and pondering its meaning through a sermon or homily, make the first room through which we pass. We 'read, mark, learn and inwardly digest' what God has to tell us. We have withdrawn, but we withdraw inside so that we may hear once more and having heard we allow that word to sink deep.

Responding and being refreshed

Having passed through the first room a curious thing occurs. We discover that the next contains a window onto the world outside. We should not yet be ready to leave but, having crossed a threshold and heard God's voice, we must respond, and the response raises two questions.

One question relates to the world outside with all its potential and problems. We have already been praying, but the tone of the prayers changes as we recognise need arising from many quarters: the world, our communities, the church itself, individuals in our care. It is a good thing to bring this need to God. Where else have we to go for life.

Yet the sheer scale of the need prompts another question. How are we to survive in a needy and contrary world when we are so far from home. We have withdrawn to commune in a particular and special way with God. While this fellowship with each other and with God is in the here-and-now, it is a reminder of God's promise that those promises are yet to be fulfilled. The fellowship of worship is a foretaste of that fulfilment and are signpost to our ultimate home. So, the celebration of the Lord's Supper soothes like a cool drink on a hot day or fills like a meal after hard labour. Indeed, the food and drink of this little meal is an outward sign by which God empowers another journey.

Renewing and returning

The second room also has a door, and we are now ready to pass this threshold. We are to return outside. We were not made to stay inside forever. Having been refreshed we are sent, renewed, into a world of desperate need.

The final words of the Anglican service sums this up as the Deacon or Lay Minister says to the congregation, 'Go in peace to love and serve the Lord' and the congregations responds, 'In the name of Christ, Amen'.

The act of corporate worship reminds us that the journey inside is only complete when we return to the outside. Having crossed the threshold of the heart and passed through the rooms which, for a time, provide a foretaste of our fulfilled home we must go back outside. The cloister which refreshes and revives must give way to the marketplace. We return sent by God to be co-workers in God's renewing work.

Breaking off and setting out

The inside-outside pattern of Christian worship embeds a 'deeply patient' theology in ordinary church life. The notion of patience in the Christian life is one that Hans Urs Von Balthasar explored at great depth. Von Balthasar is one of the most influential theologians of the

20th century, although Protestants are probably less familiar with his influence than Roman Catholics. Like Karl Barth, Von Balthasar wrote systematically and voluminously. It is a brave person to claim that they are across the work of these writers. However, the point at which I have been greatly nourished by Von Balthasar's thought is his insight into how the beauty of the formation of God's Church is part of its commendation to both itself and the world around it. Namely, the church's aesthetic quality forms part of its claim for truth.

In describing the way that a future hope informs a present patience, Von Balthasar ponders the difficult experience of the Hebrews wandering in the desert, stuck between slavery and the Promised Land. He describes their constant task as having to 'break off' from the present and 'set off' to the Promised Land.[7] Von Balthasar draws this physical experience into conversation with the tensions in the very early church to which Paul wrote, and then lays the same tension at our feet. Just as the Hebrews had to break off from their (large and complicated) camps and set off into an immediate unknown if they were to achieve the promised haven, so the church must also.

Von Balthasar does not point this out as a pragmatic necessity. Rather, as it reflects our part within God's plan. This explains why the church may be said to be 'beautiful'. When we as the church grapple with this tension, we also live-into the 'beauty' of God's work, to form us into the likeness of Jesus, here-and-now. This beauty is not a mere prettiness, rather it is a unified wholeness and fittingness. Life is seen to be 'as it should be'.

One strength of this thread, from the Exodus experience to ours, is the way that two realities are acknowledged. We are embedded in a context but not home yet. We have talked about the trap of remaining as we are and not changing until we have to. We have also pondered

---

[7] H. U. Von Balthasar, *The Glory of the Lord: A Theological Aesthetics*, trans. B. McNeil, vol. VII: Theology: The New Covenant, T & T Clark: Edinburgh, 1989, p. 485.

how easy it is to find that self-interest subverts God's gifts so that our focus remains on ourselves, whether it is us as individuals or as a close-knit group. Yet we have also celebrated the fact that God has placed us with others, whom we may delight in enriching and encouraging, as they too strive after God. We cannot live anywhere other than our present place and time. Yet, we are not complete unless we continue to 'break off and set out' toward what God has in store for us.

Earlier we noted that God's gifts will pull us away from ourselves and that, even as they are performed differently by each of us, they have the same master and the same goal. The notion behind 'goal' is that of the intended purpose. Or, that the action can and should find its completion, not simply in that it is finished, but rather as it has been filled up in much the same way that a glass is complete when it is full of your favourite beverage. For Von Balthasar, the Hebrews could not and should not escape their context because their completion was being worked-out as they broke off and set out. It would find a degree of fulfilment for sure, but even in the desert there was a purpose in not remaining as comfortable as they could manage given the circumstances. Practically this meant yearning for fullness without withdrawing from the process of being filled.

This is a deeply significant insight for us as we approach daily church life and is especially important as we ponder the tension between what seems good for us now and what will help us to be complete. In terms of Paul's sense of giftedness, being gifted means being gifted together. Being gifted together means being gifted for the other, and that is the case because we are not yet complete as a whole body. There are more to join us on the journey.

The point of being gifted is that we will seek out how to encourage and build up the others around us so that they may be whom it is that God is drawing them on to being. This is the foundation of our share in the spiritual formation or discipleship of others. Accordingly, the operation of spiritual gifts as being for the benefit of the other is the engine room of change. Even if the change is uncomfortable. Happily, it also means that we can contemplate change ahead of apparent need. That is, as I look out for what I must become I must look out for you. This is because I will then help you to identify and put in place the change that will be completed by God, and you will do the same for me.

I wonder if...?

Pal, Pam and the two Pauls would be surprised to discover that they must walk the same sandy path as the Hebrews escaping from slavery. However, this is exactly the path we tread. Like God's first people we too are called to yearn for the future while walking in the present. This strikes us most acutely when we must face how satisfied we are with the present. As we have discussed, this does not mean that we try to escape the here-and-now. It does mean that we must face up to the reality that our comfort in familiar ways here-and-now is a sign that we are not longing for the sort of completion that God desires for us.

This sense of holy dissatisfaction is a protection for the church in two ways. Firstly, it protects against complacency. As embodied beings who must live in the here-and-now, it is all too easy to seek the comfort and familiarity of the present. We become too attached to the practice of the present. This is even more so if we seem to be doing well, as we can find that comfort makes for selfishness. To be yearning for completion enables us to sit loosely with the pale comforts of the present, especially when asking how to change to enable growth. This can be a little challenging to our innate desire to settle

The second protection is easier. As people who can only dwell in the present, we wage war against living in either the past or the future. So, holy dissatisfaction provides a ward against helplessness and other worldliness. That is, it will help us to face the present, for all its possibilities, without becoming afraid of what might lurk in the future, nor mired in an imaginary world when God's plans are complete right now.

In giving us the capacity to imagine what may be possible, God has given us a surprising gift to help balance the realities of the present with a deep yearning for the future. The Godly, or God-focussed, imagination will cast itself ahead of the present to envisage how the completion, to which we are drawn, may be realised. So, for Pal, Pam and the Pauls, the simple question, 'I wonder what it would look like if .... was so?' becomes a key to unlock a misplaced satisfaction in the present. It also unlocks the places that God would have us traverse on the way to the future, and the people God is preparing to join in. Ironically, it will free us from ourselves and open-up the possibility that we may become attentive to the actual people who surround us; their needs, and how they may hear (and not simply listen) of the God who is making all things new.

The church is to be a people yearning for home without pining away. On the one hand restless and dissatisfied with the present, always up for change, seeking out any opportunity to raise up newly empowered people in the body of Christ. Yet, on the other hand, patient and steadfast in the present, looking to help spiritual roots grow deep and strong. And so we wait, with the tension. However, it is amazing the fun you can have while you are waiting!

I wonder...

1

If God could do anything here, what would it be?
Why have we chosen this?

2

What sort of change would this
work bring in/require of us?

3

How would this prepare us to be at home
in the fulfilment of God's promises?

CHAPTER THREE

Don't focus on Sunday
(or Saturday night, or Wednesday morning)

When we last visited St Silas by the Overpass, Pal was seated at the keyboard. We did not know that he had not long left the building on Saturday night before it was time to return to set up for Sunday worship. Pal takes his music seriously, and even more, he will immerse himself in the tunes and cadences of his favourite hymns until we worry that he cannot come up for air! He was so late leaving on Saturday because it took a long time to get his fingers around the tune of an unfamiliar hymn. Sunday was coming, and the pressure was on.

St Silas tends to be a bit on the formal side. Pal works hard at the music, but it is of an older style. On Saturday evening, as Pal was putting the finishing touches on his songs, The Warehouse Church across town was reverberating with the sounds of a full band rehearsing a song they had written themselves. They were practising late because the amplifiers and lights refused to work and had taken several hours to coax into life. Sunday was coming, and the pressure was on.

Great Trap 3: Thinking a 'professional' service will attract people

We may never articulate it this way, but it is easy to fall into the trap of thinking that a polished or 'professional' worship service will win people. Or, in other words, people will be attracted to what happens on Sunday morning, or evening, or Friday night, or whenever it is we gather. In some ways this is a natural thing to think. As Christians, worshipping God is vital to our being. We want to do this well. Surely a well-produced time of worship will attract others too! So, while Pal and the Worship Band practice hard to give a sacrifice of praise to God, the thought that someone from the outside will find the music (or prayers, or sermon or liturgy) irresistible is never far away. That bad note, or the missed chorus, matters because we might appear unprepared to the visitor, who may never return.

As natural as this is, thinking that a 'professional' service will attract people makes three errors. A pragmatic one, a sociological one, and a spiritual one. It is right that as churches we do not invest great amounts of our energy in analysing the productiveness of our time. In many ways worship is a divine waste of time. There is little more produced than the echoes of a song of praise wafting to God like a pleasing aroma. To seek to quantify an outcome in terms of people being attracted to the activity of worship begins an uncomfortable journey, which (if we are honest) will end in the deduction that worship is either ineffective most of the time (because people do not come and stay), or that worship exists for people and their stimulation.

The honest pragmatist will realise that a 'time versus energy versus outcome' (in terms of more people joining church) analysis will show that we put much more time and effort into our services of worship than is justified by the numbers of people who will be attracted. This is true whether the service is read from a book and comprises some judiciously chosen hymns played on an old organ, or if it is a complex and unique event delivered fresh and never repeated. Putting energy and effort into the preparation of worship is a good thing. Indeed, some may argue that it is the primary thing we must do. However, it is an error to think that if we deliver a professional or polished service people will be attracted in numbers that will justify the effort.

Sociologically, in the western world people will not simply 'walk through the door' under their own steam. In other words, the force that prompts people to visit a church and stay must be powerful enough to override the counter force that makes church attendance unthinkable. Two further aspects need to be considered to help find the reason why people would come and stay. Firstly, the cultural distance between any expression of corporate worship and the lives and norms of western people is now so great that when people do come to church, they actually expect something foreign to be happening. This means that translation of a foreign activity is our priority, rather than the provision of an immediately comfortable experience. Those who come will come despite an initial level of discomfort. Secondly, while a faith response may be garnered at an 'event' the precursors are more likely to be many personal, pastoral and discursive encounters the person has already had. These small encounters are like water priming a pump before it begins its work, or the time taken to pre-heat an oven. Seekers are attracted to church because they trust and have affection for the people with whom they have these ordinary faith-full encounters.

Spiritually, worship is primarily about God: hearing from, receiving from, and asking of, God. To make worship in the first instance about people, misplaces the necessary emphasis, and tries to manipulate an outcome. A little like a word that may be unrecognisable when mispronounced, worship that is not derived primarily from the profound pursuit of God is mispronounced. The form may be recognisable, but the misplaced motive skews its ultimate value. Any change that arises in us or others occurs coincidentally to the worshipful activity and should not be a planned or even plannable occurrence. As those charged with responsibility to worship God well, to wilfully construct our approach with the eye not fixed on God alters the activity.

All I have written is not meant to imply that worship is an insider-only activity, nor one that will be unattractive to those who experience it for the first time. Rather, the trap of seeking to attract people through worship takes our own love of worshipping God and jumps to the conclusion that if only we make it attractive others will love God too. The worship becomes the focus, not the God who is being worshipped.

'We would see Jesus'

Stand-up comedians are sometimes parodied as beginning their routines, 'a funny thing happened to me on the way here'. I find it interesting how frequently the funny things that happened to the prophets, disciples, and Jesus himself while going about everyday life turn out to change our view of the world. The coincidental relationship, between worship and people who are not yet Christian engaging with God, is illustrated powerfully through an episode in Jesus' life immediately following his triumphal entry into Jerusalem. An obvious and significant event (Jesus entering Jerusalem like a king to be crowned), gave way to something insignificant and almost forgettable.

The thing is, it was not forgotten. I suspect this was because as the disciples began their apostolic work, sent out to grow and gather the church, they reflected on this 'funny thing that happened on the way' and realised it represented certain centre of gravity when it came to worship and attracting new people.

John 12:20–26

Now among those who went up to worship at the festival were some Greeks. They came to Philip, who was from Bethsaida in Galilee, and said to him, "Sir, we wish to see Jesus." Philip went and told Andrew; then Andrew and Philip went and told Jesus. Jesus answered them, "The hour has come for the Son of Man to be glorified. Very truly, I tell you, unless a grain of wheat falls into the earth and dies, it remains just a single grain; but if it dies, it bears much fruit. Those who love their life lose it, and those who hate their life in this world will keep it for eternal life. Whoever serves me must follow me, and where I am, there will my servant be also. Whoever serves me, the Father will honor.

Despite the gathering, dark clouds of opposition and dissent Jesus is feted like a crown prince ready to take his throne. The Triumphal Entry which has begotten our annual Palm Sunday celebrations had just occurred. Strangely the people who were pictured by John in his Gospel as being a wavering and uncomprehending mass opened their mouths in praise of Jesus. Their cries of Hosanna, 'God saves,' are reinforced by 'Blessed is the one who comes in the name of the Lord!' The procession of donkeys, waving palm branches and a makeshift royal carpet all occur in direct contravention of the directives and disposition of the religious leadership. It is guerrilla worship! It is a spontaneous recognition of what God is doing and is expressed through a sophisticated, if spontaneous, ritual act.

It must have been an exciting time to have been around Jesus. The bleakness and distress of his impending doom would have lifted in one bright and luminous moment. I wonder whether the first disciples, who had reconciled themselves to sharing in the opposition Jesus faced, thought the tide had turned. Here a popular movement spoke truth to power – Jesus was indeed the Messiah. He was the blessed one who came in the name of the Lord. This was worship at its most free.

However, it is the next episode that captures my attention as a pastor. A group of Greek-speakers seek out one of the Greek-speaking disciples and ask for an audience with Jesus – 'Sir we would see Jesus'. Three things stand out for me in this slight exchange. The first is that the Greeks found someone they thought might be able to broker a meeting. The Greek-speakers found the disciple with a Greek name (Phillip) and from a Greek-speaking district to help translate the fantastic things they had seen, and broker a meeting with the man who had just been acknowledged as 'of the Lord'. The layers of significance wrapping Jesus' Triumphal Entry would have required an intuitive and deep knowledge of the Hebrew Scriptures as well as the cultural manifestation of contemporary devotional life. I wonder whether these 'outsiders' saw something in Philip, which gave them hope that the wonder they had observed may be explained, interpreted, for them.

I am then prompted to think about their approach. The grand, strange, and explicit worshipful act which they must have witnessed prompted the desire to meet Jesus. In other words, the worship was neither the terminus of the journey, nor sufficient to answer their questions. Rather it was probably the spur to prompt an active search for a conversation with Jesus. In asking Philip to be the interpreter of the strange experience, they knew that it was a personal encounter with Jesus that would straighten things out for them.

Finally, it is Jesus' ambivalence to the approach that hits home. We do not hear whether a meeting was organised. Neither do we discover the spiritual fate of the Greeks. What we do see (and hear) is Jesus declaring that a new epoch is about to dawn. That is, his reference to a seed falling into the ground to die and be fruitfully reborn refocusses us on his inevitable journey to crucifixion, but also points ahead to a new era for which this death will make way. My initial shock at what seems like a dismissal of the earnest Greeks is modified as I realise what Jesus is doing. He has just been the focus of an incredible, spontaneous act of worship, yet this is not the end point of his own ministry. In Jesus' mind there is a greater harvest to come that is intimately attached to his death and resurrection.

In this context the somewhat extraneous episode of the Greeks stands as an invitation to all who were not part of the inside group; the ones in on the secret of what it meant to worship well. There is hope for all those unable to see and say what was going on! Jesus was not only deserving of worship, but his own ministry would enable those on the outside to peer past the event and discover the person behind it all. It is as if Jesus is saying to us, 'You would see Jesus? Well observe my death and resurrection and you will'.

This episode helps to free me from placing too light a weight on worship and too heavy a burden on myself. It reminds me that worship is the heart-felt response to the God who is. Nothing more and nothing less. Yet it assures me that God is attractive enough to draw in others, and my performance is not primary.

Philip and his Greek friends do give me a clue in how to balance the desire to see new ones glimpse God's greatness and not turn worship into a performance designed to attract them. In discerning the value of a gift, and consequently the difference between response and reflection, we find balance.

A sacrifice of praise and thanksgiving

The nature of worship as a primarily 'God-ward' activity is affirmed in the construction of the service of the Lord's Supper. The words of Hebrews 13:5, 'Through Christ let us offer up a sacrifice of praise to God,' are invoked to frame the sacramental activity of sharing in the Eucharist. Unlike the services of Morning or Evening Prayer, in which the same verse may be used as the prompt to gather in God's name, the idea of presenting a sacrifice to God is included in the prayers that give thanks for God's gift to us.

Before we track the progress of the worshipper in a service of Holy Communion, it is important we see the different ways that the same verse (and idea) is deployed in the Prayers Services and the Eucharist. In Morning and Evening Prayer we are reminded that in gathering we are called to offer up praise and thanksgiving to God. The exhortation sounds like a starter's gun before a race. We are in the blocks and *'go'* as a body gathered to worship together; we must do so having been called to give thanks to a praiseworthy God.

In an Anglican construction of the Lord's Supper (another name for the Eucharist) this acknowledgement of God's praiseworthiness is turned around so that it becomes the motivation for the activity we have just (or just about) participated in. In this sense the verse functions not as a starter's gun but rather like a gem set in a fine gold ring. That is, we ask the praiseworthy God to take our activity as being embedded within God's own.

For people, as we are, with the gift and limitation of materiality, our joy in participation can distort how we understand the activity we pursue. I suspect, the more we enjoy an activity the more likely this distortion is to occur. It is easy to think that, in performing the act, we encompass the meaning of that act within ourselves. Yet the insertion of this reminder of God's ultimate praiseworthiness is a reminder that our own activity is contained within that larger and greater work already done by God.

As a theological lecturer, I enjoyed working with students to map the various services of the Prayer Book. We could do this in various ways. My favourite way was to show where our eyes were metaphorically looking at each stage of the service. Were we looking up, in adoration of God; down, as it were, to hear and take in God's voice; or around, at each other and the world within which we live? Each of these postures is present and we move from one to another eventually reaching a crescendo in the Great Thanksgiving and the Communion.

At its most basic level, the Eucharist (which literally means 'giving thanks') and the reading of scripture bracket the sermon and the intercessory prayers. In other words, we worshippers move seamlessly through hearing from God in the words of scripture, to pondering our response through the sermon, to pouring out our requests to God for each other and the world, back to receiving from God in the form of Holy Communion. The written word of scripture is echoed by the enacted word of the Eucharist. In each case we receive nurture and sustenance from God, and it is this sustenance that emboldens our hearts to bring the needs of our lives to God. The sacrifice of praise and thanksgiving we bring is that of finding ourselves willingly encased or embraced in God's activity. The gemstone of our life is displayed only as it is held, encased in the embrace of the praiseworthy God.

Horses and carts

For anyone who has been touched by the activity of worship, the idea that it would not attract people seems odd. Even more, anyone who knows the goodness of worship will know that it should be done well. For although we are to make a joyful, rather than skilful, noise to the Lord it seems wrong to wilfully make a poor noise, even if it is happy.

Lesslie Newbigin's legacy as a pastor is loved dearly in both India and the midlands of England. Many more of us know him as a missionary, missiologist and as a bishop. However, it was his instinct in relation to worship that made him loved by congregations in two very different parts of the world. And it is this instinct that helps us in one hand to hold a desire to worship well, and in the other hand to hold modesty in our aspirations for those who may come to worship. Newbigin insisted that 'the local congregation is the hermeneutic of the gospel'.[8]

For Newbigin, this was not a somewhat pompous phrase residing in an academic paper. Rather, it was his recognition that mission and worship belonged together in a very particular way. Practical experience had taught him that ordinary, locally-based Christians were the very best evangelists. He had also learned that in a world of competing choices the sufficiency of Christianity is best seen in heart-felt Christian observance.

Not long after graduating from theological college Newbigin, an Englishman, left the United Kingdom to serve as a pastor in India. As he settled and established a life in India, he discovered that the way in which he had been accustomed to presenting the Great News of Jesus to people in England made no real impact in his new country. He realised that the people he was now living with had well-examined, consistent ways of thinking about and living in the world. To simply say 'I have a better way for you to live' was worse than ineffective, it was laughable. Ironically, he found many people very happy to discuss Jesus' life, claims and death. He even found that many of those were attracted to Jesus, but not really interested at all in Christianity.

Rather than concluding that Christianity had nothing to offer, he was convinced that Jesus is the clue to understanding all human history and endeavour. He realised that something

---

[8] L. Newbigin, *Trinitarian Doctrine for Today's Mission*. Paternoster Press: Carlisle, 1998, pp. 27–29 (lit.: *hermeneutic* – 'when translated', i.e. interprets)

more than a mere declaration of a position was needed. In other words, people could not be *argued* into God's Kingdom. What was simultaneously respectful to those who already had a view of the world, empowering of Indian Christians, and effective in allowing people to see, understand and embrace Jesus, was to set the local church free to worship well without looking over their shoulders at anyone else. Yet this was paired with activity by which those same Christian locals were sent out as evangelists to simply tell of what God has done though Jesus.

By pairing the declaration of God's activity with the activity of worship that was not overly concerned with attracting others, each congregation allowed folk to see and hear what its members were on about. The local congregation was a microcosm of the message that the evangelists spoke. When the evangelists told of a God who forgave, the watching communities could see Christian people forgiving each other and asking an unseen God to wash away their own sins. When the evangelists taught of God's grace, the watching communities could see Christian people speaking encouraging words to each other (rather than tearing each other down) and receiving forgiveness from that same unseen God. When the evangelists assured them of God's capacity to supply their need for life as a Body in Christ, they could observe the weekly celebration of a 'little meal' which, though insufficient to nourish the body, evidently nourished the soul. While not designed to attract people, the ordinary act of local worship allowed a watching community to see what the evangelists were telling.

Ironically, by not setting out to attract others, these little congregations were very attractive because their activity made sense of the Gospel. If the congregations had sought to draw others in through the worship, they would have put the cart before the horse.

Being attractive without trying to attract

Both Pal and the band from the Warehouse Church are on to something. There is not much in life better than being lost in the divine waste of time that is worshipping God. To be gifted in being able to lead others in this wonderful invitation is a privilege and should be a joy. It is right that Pal and the band spent hours preparing and getting ready to help us less musically-gifted ones to join in. So, the pressure they all felt was symptomatic of a trap that is easy to fall in to: recognising the inherent loveliness of worship and then feeling the pressure to attract others by it.

If we can summarise this chapter, it would be to say that worship is responding to God's gift to us, and then living like it matters. As recipients of a gift worshippers are supremely uninterested in what others may think because they are primarily interested in responding to the gift giver. Music, liturgy, ritual, preaching and praying are all important in portraying the richness of the Christian life, but they are all expressions of what makes that life attractive rather than the other way around. As part of the response of the congregation to the God who has called them into relationship with each other, with Christ and, through Christ, with God's self, the worship is attractive in the same way as a picture of a mango is attractive when compared to the fruit. The worship is a foretaste of the one who is much bigger and more beautiful. There is a big difference between being attractive and trying to be attractive!

Being uninterested in what others think does not mean that we are to be insensitive to how they may receive what we are doing. There is little that is attractive in an entirely incomprehensible activity. For many, the slip, from valuing the attractiveness of worship to hoping for worship to attract others, begins when we see someone confused by what is occurring when we worship. Confusion, or worse, misunderstanding, does not help those who might be tempted to consider the claims that Jesus may have on their life. However, a helpful way of navigating this dilemma, between uninterest in the views of others and care that worship is not incomprehensible, is to change the language of attraction to that of translation.

I think that the Greek speakers sought out Philip so he could help them 'translate' what went on during Jesus' entry into Jerusalem on the very first Palm Sunday. Lesslie Newbigin understood how worship that set local Christians free to respond to the God who had given them Jesus inevitably opened opportunities for translation of what was going on in the church, so that it made sense in onlookers' own lives. One way to picture this is through the idea of putting windows in the walls of the church building. The building itself may need to be modified to accommodate the windows, but it does not need to be knocked down. However, these new windows are not to allow those inside to look out, rather they exist so that those on the outside may look in. We have seen that worship is, in many ways, an activity for insiders. But it is an activity that we insiders find supremely fulfilling because it sums up the goodness and greatness of God. Surely others will want to see and partake in this.

A more productive question than 'how can we make worship attractive to others?' is then, 'how can we enable others to look in on our worship?'. This question frees us to worship God as is fitting, as a response to God and not others, and ask what those others may perceive while they watch at the same time. It also frees us to attend to simpler, less contentious, and more productive activities alongside whatever is happening on Sunday. The connection between each of us as worshippers and others as interested onlookers is strengthened, releasing the value in those things that will allow those others to look in on the worship on their own terms.

So, four things will go a long way to helping translate exactly what it is that Christians do when they worship the good and great God.

1. **An invitation**: 'Why don't you come with me? I'd like you to come'.
2. **Patience**: The person you are inviting already has a life and a series of assumptions about what makes this life worthwhile. They will need you to give them time to 'just look'.
3. **Conversation**: Most people who do not come to church expect 'churchy' things to happen there. It is a bit odd of us to think that we can change anything so that it is immediately comprehensible and comfortable. Conversation over a coffee is the best way to help others learn the language of worship.
4. **Conviction**: If our worship is supposed to be a response to a good and great God then hypocrisy or half-heartedness really says, 'I don't actually think that God is all that worthwhile. It's good for a laugh, but it does not run deep'. What is happening in our lives between Monday and Saturday to declare that God really is good?

Here are three questions to ask
as we seek to worship well:

1
***

What is it about God that should be driving our worship?
How do I need to be reminded of this?
How should I be seeking out God's nurture
so that I can live like this?

2
***

What do we do that may look and sound foreign to
someone observing from the outside?
How might I need to translate it?

3
***

Where will the people in my community
get the chance to 'see Jesus'?
How can I help them meet Jesus?

CHAPTER FOUR

Grasp your calling

St Silas' has always struggled with a sense of inferiority, especially since the overpass went in. It was easy to be overlooked. Life was busy, the marketplace was crowded and finding an event to cut through the noise was taxing. As we know, St Silas by the Overpass really did want to reach out to the people around them, but they constantly found their message drowned out by others. Often it was the loud and powerful messages found in the media and society at large that were overwhelming. Sometimes the noise came from nearby churches, which seemed to be able to find just the right hook to draw people in.

The Warehouse Church appeared to be much better at cutting through. They always had an interesting speaker lined up, or exciting activity ready to roll. Occasionally the speaker or activity chosen by The Warehouse Church worried some of St Silas' older parishioners, but no-one could argue with the results. This became the topic of conversation at the local inter-church prayer group following each event. Yet the prayer group could not escape the conclusion that if all their congregations were to have their voices heard above the din made by all the alternatives, something striking had to be done.

Great Trap 4: Finding a 'hook' to get people in

Marketing and brand recognition are influential aspects of the world within which we live. We are accustomed to an environment dripping with messages designed to pique our appetites and capture our interest. And this is amplified as products compete for our attention. So, we do not simply live in a time in which communication is polished and slick, but where we also expect the perfected product to outdo its competitors. We live in a 'marketplace' where almost everything is reduced to a brand that vies for the loyalty of our souls.

It is not surprising then that both The Warehouse Church and St Silas have begun to compete in this marketplace. Without even realising it, both churches have begun to fall for the trap of seeking out just the right 'hook' to get people in. Or, in other words, marketing their churches and the Christian message in just the right way so that others will be tempted to visit, stop, and stay. There are four problems with this approach, which have the potential to undermine any deep spiritual growth, even if the hook is successful in landing an enquirer or two.

Approaching the way we present ourselves to the world as a marketing exercise runs the risk of destroying the trust of the very people whose faith we hope will grow. As a youth-group leader, I was aware how easy it was to attract a crowd, but I was also aware how hard it was to then communicate and share what it meant to follow Jesus. This was because the things I could promise to entice the young people suddenly seemed unrelated to the actual event as I sought to promote engagement with God's word and God's people. The young people who had come in response to an enticement were resentful when it became something else. To bait a hook expressly to attract a person to church will likely mean that the appealing feature will not be a core and lovely part of Christian life. To then switch the bait for hearing, learning and growing in Jesus feels like a deception. At the least, deception breeds mistrust, at its worst resentment.

A second problem with this approach is the lack of confidence shown in the 'pioneer and perfector of our faith' (Hebrews 12:2). The approach that looks for a hook to draw people in will usually prioritise something other than a consideration of Jesus. Furthermore, it will latch on to something that flashes and burns brightly at the cost of a long and enduring light. By its nature an event or message designed to shine more brightly than all the alternatives will flare and fade. The effect of this misplaced faith, in something other than Jesus and the Church, will be that those who seem to have been 'hooked' begin their life of faith without a firm foothold on the one who will perfect it.

Hooks designed to 'get people in' will often rely on a misplaced celebrity, which devalues the saints of God. The nature of momentary attraction is that the unusual, physically attractive or obviously talented will predominate. This means that when thinking of an attractive event or presentation we will utilise people whose Christian faith is not their primary attribute but rather their accomplishments, personality or beauty. In other words, it is the personal attribute of celebrity that we rely on, rather than anything intrinsic to God's great work. This devalues the witness of ordinary people who have been ennobled and empowered by God. In being brought into God's family, the ordinary saints, who inhabit the church as it is, are the ones empowered to provide a lasting witness.

If one way of finding a 'hook' is by relying on celebrity, a further way is to present ordinary Christians empty of their Christian attribute. Some attempts to catch hold of people's attention follow the line that Christians are normal, fun, or exciting – just like the world around them. These approaches relegate God to the margins and supplant God-talk or a thorough-going Christian life with a lifestyle designed to ape that which is presented elsewhere.

Yet the impulse to reach out and share the great news of God with others does require that we interact in a world full of ideas and competing messages. It is ironic that the very means God has given the church to interact with this world looks less like a hook that must compete with all the other hooks in the ocean, and more like you and me.

'As the Father has sent me, I send you'

Jesus' resurrection was heralded by distress, fear, and great anxiety. Mary Magdalene (and some of the other women who made up the band of disciples) made a tearful journey to embalm Jesus' body. The men were locked in a room afraid of the ruling parties. All of them were bewildered at the shuddering end to their hopes and dreams.

This uncertain situation was occurring after Jesus' had been raised. In other words, Mary and the others were distressed and afraid even though Jesus was alive! There is a clear and pregnant pause in the gospel narrative during which we the readers, who are so familiar with the whole story, forget that those living through it were yet to discover their place in a world which had changed. For indeed it had.

Jesus was no longer dead. The powerful forces of this world had conspired against him, had seemed to have won but, as we know, had failed. Yet, those first distressed, fearful, and anxious disciples did not know this. They thought they had nothing, even as they had everything.

John 20

Early on the first day of the week, while it was still dark, Mary Magdalene came to the tomb and saw that the stone had been removed from the tomb. So she ran and went to Simon Peter and the other disciple, the one whom Jesus loved, and said to them, "They have taken the Lord out of the tomb, and we do not know where they have laid him." Then Peter and the other disciple set out and went toward the tomb. The two were running together, but the other disciple outran Peter and reached the tomb first. He bent down to look in and saw the linen wrappings lying there, but he did not go in. Then Simon Peter came, following him, and went into the tomb. He saw the linen wrappings lying there, and the cloth that had been on Jesus' head, not lying with the linen wrappings but rolled up in a place by itself. Then the other disciple, who reached the tomb first, also went in, and he saw and believed; for as yet they did not understand the scripture, that he must rise from the dead. Then the disciples returned to their homes. But Mary stood weeping outside the tomb. As she wept, she bent over to look into the tomb; and she saw two angels in white, sitting where the body of Jesus had been lying, one at the head and the other at the feet. They said to her, "Woman, why are you weeping?" She said to them, "They have taken away my Lord, and I do not know where they have laid him." When she had said this, she turned around and saw Jesus standing there, but she did not know that it was Jesus.

Jesus said to her, "Woman, why are you weeping? Whom are you looking for?" Supposing him to be the gardener, she said to him, "Sir, if you have carried him away, tell me where you have laid him, and I will take him away." Jesus said to her, "Mary!" She turned and said to him in Hebrew, "Rabbouni!" (which means Teacher). Jesus said to her, "Do not hold on to me, because I have not yet ascended to the Father. But go to my brothers and say to them, 'I am ascending to my Father and your Father, to my God and your God.'" Mary Magdalene went and announced to the disciples, "I have seen the Lord"; and she told them that he had said these things to her. When it was evening on that day, the first day of the week, and the doors of the house where the disciples had met were locked for fear of the Jews, Jesus came and stood among them and said, "Peace be with you." After he said this, he showed them his hands and his side. Then the disciples rejoiced when they saw the Lord. Jesus said to them again, "Peace be with you. As the Father has sent me, so I send you." When he had said this, he breathed on them and said to them, "Receive the Holy Spirit. If you forgive the sins of any, they are forgiven them; if you retain the sins of any, they are retained." But Thomas (who was called the Twin), one of the twelve, was not with them when Jesus came. So the other disciples told him, "We have seen the Lord." But he said to them, "Unless I see the mark of the nails in his hands, and put my finger in the mark of the nails and my hand in his side, I will not believe." A week later his disciples were again in the house, and Thomas was with them. Although the doors were shut, Jesus came and stood among them and said, "Peace be with you." Then he said to Thomas, "Put your finger here and see my hands. Reach out your hand and put it in my side. Do not doubt but believe." Thomas answered him, "My Lord and my God!" Jesus said to him, "Have you believed because you have seen me? Blessed are those who have not seen and yet have come to believe." Now Jesus did many other signs in the presence of his disciples, which are not written in this book. But these are written so that you may come to believe that Jesus is the Messiah, the Son of God, and that through believing you may have life in his name.

Mary's first encounter with the risen Jesus (John 20:13–17) is at once a flash of exciting brilliance and ambivalence. How could the same figure who greeted her so kindly refuse an embrace and send her away?

Mary was the first to hear the words of commission that would begin to make sense of the newness which was beginning to dawn on a world held captive to death. As Mary was sent back to the frightened disciples hiding away in a locked room she was also sent to 'tell them what he had said to her' (John 20:18).

As the new life first experienced by Jesus crept into our world, Mary was recruited as both witness and apostle. This pattern was to be repeated when, having heard Mary's surprising news, the still fearful disciples came face to face with Jesus in his resurrected life. Their fear gave way to joy, but this joy still needed the assurance of peace. Both the news and reality of Jesus alive-through-death was of such enormity that fear and confusion nevertheless clung to their experience. Bearing witness to earth shattering events inevitably carried a mystifying sense of bewilderment. As the first to see and hear Jesus, Mary and the disciples sat at the prow of a ship setting into new seas. It was little wonder that the assurance of peace was needed.

This pattern was repeated, albeit in a slightly different form, when Jesus met Thomas who had previously been absent. Repeating his assurance of peace, Jesus insisted that Thomas physically handle him. We can read this as Jesus' confrontation of Thomas' doubt. However,

I think that it is entirely consistent with the action to understand Jesus' insistence on touch as an act of restoration. In spite of Thomas' doubt, he is included in this first band of witnesses. He is given special assurance that Jesus is indeed real and no ghostly manifestation. Thomas' grateful belief opens the way for his inclusion in the apostolic call, which Mary and the other disciples had heard before him.

Before seeing Thomas, when standing before the disciples in the locked room, Jesus had moved directly from the restoration of his peace to a commission. Noticing this movement is vital if we are to grasp the nature of our engagement as the church with the life of the Trinity and the world in which we live. In a simple phrase, 'As the Father has sent me, I send you', Jesus does two things. He places his incredible life brought-forth-through death in direct continuity with the commission he had received from the first person of the Trinity, the Father. His gentle, restorative appearance to Mary and the company of disciples, was part of his being sent by the Father. Jesus then places the disciples in a position of incredible honour in similar continuity with the Father. Thomas' inclusion in this call, after the fact, only serves to underline that God was calling a depleted and doubtful mob into a primary position of importance in his plan.

To bear witness to the risen Jesus is not the same as bearing witness to a nuclear explosion. Neither is it the same as discussing the fluctuations of the stock market portrayed on the news. The blinding flash of the blast of a nuclear explosion overwhelms any engagement. Its overpowering nature reduces those who behold the flash to mere bystanders and there is no engagement in anything outside the source of the blast. On the other hand, the value of the equities market as it is shown on the ticker beneath a television news program arrives as a bald set of numbers. Self-evident and without sanction. We might discuss them over a coffee. We may even debate and commend their relative merits. However, we do not participate in the base value ascribed to each stock.

In deciding not to display himself in the blinding glory befitting the one who had been raised a victor from death, Jesus chose another way. He engaged the distressed, fearful and anxious as witnesses. Furthermore, Jesus then laid upon them the awesome privilege of being sent into the world to pass on his message of resurrection. That same generous gentleness, which Jesus showed to the first frightened ones, he constantly gives to our world. He neither overwhelms nor removes participation. Rather Jesus continues to engage those who, like Mary and the other disciples, are often weak and vulnerable: 'As the Father has sent me, so I send you!' (John 20:21b).

Go in peace to love and serve the Lord

The same movement – from witnessing the fruit of Jesus' resurrection to being sent to bear out its significance in the every-day world – is heard in the final words of dismissal at the end of a service of gathered worship. Typically, the service leader will proclaim, 'Go in peace to love and serve the Lord' and the congregation will respond, 'In the name of Christ, Amen'. The dismissal may be accompanied by ritual, it may be said as an afterthought to be disposed of prior to the morning tea, and it may even be forgotten altogether. However, a few things are worth noting about this impulse to end a time of gathered worship with a formal dismissal into ordinary life.

The performance of this couplet links gathered liturgical worship with individual daily godliness, which is worship in another mode. Our modern way of talking about what we 'do in church' as worship has the tendency to downplay, or make us forget, that what we 'do outside church' should also be an expression of our love and devotion to God. Which is, of course, worship as well. To be sent out to love and serve the Lord links a gathered and specific expression of love and devotion to a more individualised and personal lifetime of worship.

Similarly, this dismissal is the explicit connexion between the nurture provided by Christ and our role in telling out the grand story of his life, death, resurrection and continuing reign. In gathering to hear from God and receive sustenance from his hand we are in fact beholding God's great work again. The words of Scripture – read aloud, then pondered and explained in the sermon – along with the Lord's Supper – enacted and consumed by the congregation – form a disciplined and blessed space in which God's acts are seen and heard once more. The dismissal marks the movement from passive to active witness. We have witnessed what God has done, and now we go and bear witness to others.

When the dismissal is enacted with a full sense of its liturgical possibilities, the interplay between receiving nurture from God and hearing his apostolic call shines bright. In situations where the service leader may be different from the preacher and the president of the Lord's Supper, the hinge connecting nurture and mission is amplified. This is particularly so if the service leader is a deacon or lay person. In having a voice that represents the ministry of the church outside the gathering (through a deacon) or the whole people of God (through a lay person) the priestly acts of nurture through the sermon and Supper are taken by the whole and then sent forth into the world. That is, the nurture of God's people reaches its ultimate purpose when it is visibly active in their every-day lives. This voice is given a performative value when the dismissal is announced from the rear of the church building or immediately prior to a symbolic procession out. As actors in a divine drama, we stand at the threshold of a new scene and stride through with purpose.

So, go!

Whose mission?

We read about Lesslie Newbigin in the previous chapter: particularly his sense that the 'local congregation is the hermeneutic of the Gospel'. Ultimately this recognition of the value of the ordinary, usually small and struggling, congregations grew from his sense that we are a mission with a people, not people with a mission. This is another way of saying that our calling to be and do things emanates from a prior being and doing. We are and we do because we are sent out from God. This rather startling reality is quite different from the way we often think about mission.

Mission is usually framed as an expression of what we want to do: our desires or best sense of the purpose of an organisation. It is usually expressed as discrete activities that are distinct to the core of our being. We 'have' a mission, we 'do' acts of mission. Rarely do we think of ourselves as 'being' mission. This is because to think of ourselves as 'being' mission requires the controlling hand to be not our own. Newbigin reminds us that we are God's mission. It is God who sends, and it is God who determines the shape and priority of our life.

The heart of the Christian life is to bear witness to the magnificent acts of God. This is done in three ways. The most diffuse is through the personal testimony of how God has been active to sustain and grow each of us as individuals. No Christian is without the capacity to tell out what it is that God has done to open their eyes to his truth and 'do good' by in their own experience. In this sense we can talk about the way that God is working all things out for our good (see Romans 8:28). The next tier is through the magnificence of God's creation. There are times when we can only gaze in wonder as the manifold beauty of what is around us shines forth. The fruitful complexity of the natural world invites us to become engaged. To eat and enjoy, to dig and to plant, to trek and to discover: all open new doorways to enjoy God's handiwork. Ironically even the travail and destruction of the created order provides opportunity to point out God's greatness. The very fact that our hearts break bespeaks the marvel of what should be (see Romans 8:22-23).

Most of all, we can draw our personal experience of life and the common experience within the world into sharp relief as we tell and re-tell that Jesus has risen from the dead. For Newbigin this was news that created an 'explosion of joy'. While our personal testimony cannot be argued with because it is ours to own, it can be dismissed as wrong-headed or a crutch. Similarly, the glory we ascribe to God when awestruck by creation can be explained away or attributed to other causes. Jesus' resurrection from the dead stands as the unique intervention of God in space and time to reverse that which had previously been inevitable. One may deny that it occurred, but one cannot explain away its magnitude. When God raised Jesus from the dead the natural trajectory of the world was arrested (Romans 8:38). God's action did not rely on us, nor does it stand in need of our validation. It does stand, for those who recognise it, as changing everything.

Many years have passed since these earth-shattering events. We who follow on after Jesus, do so at a distance. Mary and the other disciples, who saw the resurrected Jesus first, were dramatically recruited into a way of life that went beyond the transmission of information. They were called to share in a life that had its origin in God: a life made active as it was sent out to be in the world that God was redeeming. They were a living witness to God's dramatic and history-changing power. Yet they did this in-and-through the ordinary aspects of daily life.

The amazing thing is that we too are 'sent ones'. We share in the apostolic call. We find ourselves sent out by Jesus. So, while we live at a distance from the time of Jesus' resurrection, we are not far when it comes to his person. Our call is both continuous with those first eyewitnesses, and relationally immediate. As the Father had sent Jesus, so Jesus sends the disciples in the upper room, and us! Our challenge, in heeding the re-presentation of the risen Jesus as handed down from Mary and the others, is to inhabit, as they did, the life that Jesus himself made freely available.

In hearing the explosion of joy from those first disciples we have witnessed what God has done. We witness as bystanders who cannot change what has occurred: but not as a bystander who can walk away to resume an everyday life. We, like the first disciples, have been drawn into God's own life and, in being part of that life, may now go and bear witness to others.

Humility

As we return to St Silas it is easy to share their sense that they are being left behind by a world, and other churches, that simply have a better product to sell. However, the reminder that we are sent to not simply share a message but to inhabit God's life, opens great possibilities for even weak and dispirited congregations.

The importance of the shape of our individual and corporate life cannot be understated. Knowing the ruler of all, from whom life flows and who has ennobled us by sending us on his business, should shape who we are. While what we know about Christianity is important, the one whom we know is central. In other words, we do not truly know what it means to be a Christian unless we exist in relationship with Jesus who is sent from God.

The wonderfully surprising thing is that even as this demands the utter reconfiguration of our life, being drawn into the deep knowing of relationship means that we are given the treasure of the very being of God. The primary way in which we may then pass on this life, is through the words that disclose God's self. The gift of Scripture is that

God has not left us groping in the dark, uncertain of our approach, but, as the words of Scripture show us the incarnate Word of his Son – Jesus, we may approach life with extraordinary confidence. We bear the very words of the author of life!

Lest this confidence go to our head, being the 'sent ones' means that our confidence rests solely on the one who spoke first. Our role is a humble one. We are but emissaries. In the world, humility and confidence are an unusual mix. Usually humility is joined to a servile demeanour, and confidence is attended by brash self-confidence. Yet we who are sent out by Jesus, who was sent by the Father, carry the capacity to pass on the words of life, and life to the full, without the need to make something of ourselves. We are set free from a thrusting confidence because God has already done so much more for us than we could hope. God has given us his life.

The key task, when thinking about how it is that others may come to join the church (or more to the point follow Jesus), is how we may follow our calling. Rather than finding a hook, which may snag a person or two, our primary direction is to be a people who exude a faith-filled life. This does not excuse standoffishness or aggression but allows us to show others the primacy and sufficiency of God. When our faith is so idiosyncratic or aggressive that people cannot make head nor tail of what we espouse, this is the spur to examine what it is we bear – for it should be light and life. When our faith is so far off or distant that people cannot come close, this should inspire us to move closer. Holding our 'sentness' dear means that, rather than desperately focusing on what may attract others, we may allow others to come and, like toddlers learning to play in a sandpit, 'play alongside' us at life. In playing alongside others, they will be able to share in the benefits of Christian hope, gaining a taste for the goodness that flows from God.

So, look for opportunities to grow alongside people in relationship. Rather than searching for just the right event to tease a passing eye, try out activities such as a walking club, an open reading time for young parents and their toddlers, a regular coffee meet. Activities such as these not only enable conversation in which God-talk can flow, but also allow for continual contact, which empowers others to see the sufficiency of God's life. Even the smallest of churches can do this.

Here are three questions to ask
as we 'be' God's mission:

1

In what ways may people look at me and my congregation
and be able to see and hear God?

2

In the interactions I have, how can I deliver the message
of God's great work in the world? Where do I lose
opportunities because I am too shy or too brash?

3

How do I rehearse who God is and practise living
a 'God shaped life'? In what ways do I participate
in God's concerns?

CHAPTER FOUR

CHAPTER FIVE

Don't try too hard!

Pam makes a great morning tea. Every Sunday. She has no equal in the known universe, and those who visit St Silas remember her sponge cakes and the veritable cornucopia of slices with delight. The morning tea has become a wonderful place to share deep fellowship. Visitors are warmly welcomed, and the regular congregation has the unusual distinction of staying on well after the service has finished. They love to talk and pray together. It is a real point of hospitality and an intentional part of their congregational life.

Every week the feast arrives early, even before most of the congregation. Usually, I am the only one who sees Pam slowly carrying each basket and box in from her car, methodically arranging the table and preparing the accompanying dishes. Yet even I do not see the Sunday preparations actually beginning on Tuesday, when the weekly shop includes the requirements for the baking schedule.

Pam has been doing this for years. She began when her own children were at home and Peter was still alive, but that was a long time ago. She still believes this to be an act of service and realises how helpful the preparations are in encouraging people to stay, sit and share. Even though it is getting hard, Pam feels that this is the one thing she can do to keep the church's doors open. If there were no morning tea would anyone come?

Great Trap 5: If we try hard enough, we will get back on a sustainable footing...then everything will be okay

It is easy for us to align reaching out to others or serving people in ministry with the capacity to organise ourselves easily or pay for the various costs that go with church life and ministry. Yet, this is like comparing apples and oranges. Both apples and oranges belong in the fruit bowl but are quite distinct fruits. Of course, serving people in ministry and organising ourselves sustainably do have some connection. After all, if we cannot release people to devote their time to ministry and outreach, and if we cannot provide safe and well-functioning facilities in which to gather, then the numbers of people who can be served are limited. However, if we approach the question of what we do as church (our activities) as the way to underpin or prop up our organisation, we mistake matters of sustainable organisation for those of fruitfulness in life.

For those of us like Pam, who have worked hard to reach out to others and nurture the spiritual life of our congregations, weariness can become the driver of this mistaken alignment. This is ironic because the reason we have been so active is usually a clear and heart-felt focus on the wellbeing and growth of others. It is also insidious, as our tiredness will creep up on us until we catch ourselves thinking, 'I'll do this for one more year and then we will have earned enough money to employ a kids' worker', or 'I'll persevere with the morning teas until some of the young ones step up and take over'. Whether ironic or insidious, we can too easily find ourselves thinking of our acts of Christian service as the means to an institutional end, rather than the expression of a God-shaped life. The sustainability of our congregation, instead of the growth of those we serve, becomes primary.

We need not be surprised by this slippage. Christianity is not solitary, rather it is a relational faith. We are called to be together with others. As soon as we must relate to others, we must also face organisational questions. How will we spend our collective energy? How will we prioritise our resources? Where will we meet? How do we keep each other safe? Who will attend to our diet of teaching and pattern of worship? How will we engage with others? Who will clean the building and check the gutters? These questions must all be thought through, and the answers agreed upon. However, if these answers make the funding of positions or facilities, or the provision of hands to do the work, the end point of our corporate life, then we have inadvertently switched to a model of church which places its self-sustenance ahead of other priorities.

I can remember falling into this trap myself as I sought to lead a fine congregation in outreach to the local community. We had many things happening within the life of the church. Indeed, all the usual activities you would expect from a healthy church could be found on our promotional material. Except one. An effective outreach to the local community was missing, so I determined to begin one. And we did. Every fourth Sunday evening, our church provided a community meal. People came from both congregation and community. But as the months went by, my wife and I found ourselves the only ones preparing the food, setting up the facility, planning the activities, and then cleaning up. It was hard work, and I became resentful. This was our initiative to 'top-up' the evening service once more so that we had a viable offering.

Gladly, before I complained to the congregation, I realised that the others were also tired. These same folks were run off their feet doing all the other things a busy church should do. So I made the best ministry decision of my life. We stopped everything else! Well, not quite everything, but most things. It was vital, at this stage of our church life, that we reengaged with our community, so we paused many of our groups and duties. Released from their busyness, the congregation became willing helpers and (most importantly) hospitable to their neighbours. Our website did not look so good, with many of our activities in furlough, but we entered a season of fruitful growth. Christians and non-Christians alike ate, talked and shared a vision of God together that we could not have done if we had continued trying to make things happen.

Treasure in jars of clay

The Apostle Paul is often regarded as the 'systematiser' of the Christian faith. But what may be overlooked is that his surviving writings were responses to pastoral and missional need. In other words, Paul's response to the requirements and opportunities of ministry displayed skilful living, in which the shape of a God-ward life informed and filled his response. This meant that he could answer the needs of the time and place in flexible and creative ways that flowed from a consistently internalised set of values.

2 Corinthians 4

Therefore, since it is by God's mercy that we are engaged in this ministry, we do not lose heart. We have renounced the shameful things that one hides; we refuse to practice cunning or to falsify God's word; but by the open statement of the truth we commend ourselves to the conscience of everyone in the sight of God. And even if our gospel is veiled, it is veiled to those who are perishing. In their case the god of this world has blinded the minds of the unbelievers, to keep them from seeing the light of the gospel of the glory of Christ, who is the image of God. For we do not proclaim ourselves; we proclaim Jesus Christ as Lord and ourselves as your slaves for Jesus' sake. For it is the God who said, "Let light shine out of darkness," who has shone in our hearts to give the light of the knowledge of the glory of God in the face of Jesus Christ. But we have this treasure in clay jars, so that it may be made clear that this extraordinary power belongs to God and does not come from us. We are afflicted in every way, but not crushed; perplexed, but not driven to despair; persecuted, but not forsaken; struck down, but not destroyed; always carrying in the body the death of Jesus, so that the life of Jesus may also be made visible in our bodies. For while we live, we are always being given up to death for Jesus' sake, so that the life of Jesus may be made visible in our mortal flesh. So death is at work in us, but life in you. So we do not lose heart. Even though our outer nature is wasting away, our inner nature is being renewed day by day. For this slight momentary affliction is preparing us for an eternal weight of glory beyond all measure, because we look not at what can be seen but at what cannot be seen; for what can be seen is temporary, but what cannot be seen is eternal. But just as we have the same spirit of faith that is in accordance with scripture—"I believed, and so I spoke"—we also believe, and so we speak, because we know that the one who raised the Lord Jesus will raise us also with Jesus, and will bring us with you into his presence. Yes, everything is for your sake, so that grace, as it extends to more and more people, may increase thanksgiving, to the glory of God.

It is significant that Paul begins this chapter, which concludes so strongly with an exposition of hope, by grounding his present experience in God's mercy. Ministry is foundational to his lived experience. Yet ministry is a gift given by God and, as we will see, it is empowered by God's activity.

Paul quickly progresses his discussion in chapter 4 to expose a way of understanding the work that looks through the lens of Jesus' redemptive activity. That is, God pre-empts Paul's own knowledge, so that Paul may correctly see Jesus Christ, who in turn enables the deep knowing of relational intimacy with God. Where Paul's experience of life is founded on God's mercy, this mercy begets knowledge.

The vulnerability Paul displays in 2 Corinthians 4 arises clearly from the ministry that has flowed from a renewed vision of God through the face of Christ. Verses 7 to 12 are a rehearsal of Paul's qualifications for ministry and give a stunning glimpse into his way of life. The dense phrasing, in which a negative experience is brought into parallel with a positive work of God, builds upon itself to the conclusion.

> For we who are living are always being handed over unto death because of Jesus, so that the life of Jesus may be made clear in our mortal flesh. Accordingly death is made active in us and life in you! (2 Corinthians 4:11–12)

Through the presentation of God's enabling power working in-and-through Paul's own weakness, Paul lays the forward-looking foundation for his life. Ministry, the very expression of Paul's action-informed-by-mercy, is enabled by the power of God rather than the strength of humanity. This means that weakness is no hindrance to effective life, rather it is the ground upon which skilled living occurs. Furthermore, the ministry lived in weakness and vulnerability demonstrates a forward vision that enables action in the present. This is because partaking in weakness, following Jesus' own dying, foreshadows and brings into the present the experience of resurrected life, whose consummation lies in the future.

Paul's primary goal is the glorification of God. Yet this primary goal is worked out through the participation of the people of Corinth in the mercy of God, which is seen in thanksgiving. Paul's aim, then, is to participate in '… the knowledge of the glory of God in the face of Jesus Christ' (2 Cor 4:6). Paul does this through helping others 'know' also. In this way, the inward renewal experienced in-and-through 'the light and momentary troubles' of the present-day bear witness to the unseen, but eternal 'weight of glory'.

Not unlike us, Paul was navigating life within a context that bore influence from multiple sources. His 'first' world was that of a Roman citizen living within a Hellenic culture. This was the dominant atmosphere of Corinth, a busy, successful commercial town physically located in Greece but acting as the meeting place of Europe and Asia. It was the proverbial 'melting pot' of the Roman Empire but was shaped clearly by foundational Greek values. Yet within the Corinthian church, Paul was also interacting with an expression of Jewish culture that had itself mixed with the dominant Greco-Roman milieu. As with the 'first' world, this 'second' world was not unfamiliar to Paul (compare with Acts 21:39 and Phil 3:4–6). He had lived in both. Yet his attachment to Christ, and the vision that flowed from this relationship, meant that Paul was able to interact with these two worlds.

In underlining the mercy of his calling, Paul turns the attention of the congregation away from himself towards Jesus, who is the image of the glory of God. Whatever Paul says is intended to highlight Jesus' sufficiency in bringing people to God. In this sense, Paul is not unlike announcers backing offstage as they indicate the arrival of the star performer. Therefore, Paul interprets his obvious show of weakness (2 Cor 4:7–11, 5:1–5, 11:21–33) as God's performance ground. It seems he is quite happy to be weak in this way so that restored relationship may be achieved.

Paul's interaction with the Corinthian church was fraught with difficulty. The presence of the dominant culture was complicated by the presence of aggressive interlopers who directly questioned Paul's fitness to lead the community. This was not a detached, impersonal affair: it challenged him personally. It would have been easy for Paul to either withdraw from relationship, and therefore ministry with the Corinthians, or to respond to the challenges in kind. However he chose not to. Rather, he drew upon his attachment to Christ, and Christ's dying, to challenge what the Christian community in Corinth was accepting in their leadership. Paul's robust faith in God's power to lift up his weakness enabled him extraordinary durability and focus even when he seemed worn out and at wits-end.

Honest with God

I love the Great Litany from the Book of Common Prayer. I discovered it first when leafing through a facsimile of the first two drafts of an English language prayer book compiled by Thomas Cranmer, which became the backbone of all the others that followed. A litany really is just a list. In this case a list of prayers, each with a response. The service leader will pray a short prayer and the congregation will respond with a line, making the prayer theirs too. The Great Litany is the longest of these prayer-lists. I find that the Great Litany makes me pray for things that I would not normally think to pray for. This is especially so for aspects of my life and spiritual health that are foreign to our modern context. Things like my own tendency toward vain-glory and hypocrisy.

There is an honesty in this kind of prayer. It is certainly an inward honesty, for who of us can claim to truly be without hypocrisy. However, the point of the prayer-list is that this honesty is before God. Our own integrity is not the end point, rather the goal is to be honest with God. We tend to be better at spotting the faults and failings of others than of ourselves, so a spur to honest self-reflection is a rare gift. This gift is amplified by its location within a prayer. We certainly do need to own the vulnerabilities that are laid bare, yet we do so in God's presence.

There is a wonderfully restorative power that comes when confronting our failure before God. This is because God delights to forgive wrong and then make new. In other words, the integrity in this honest admission of fault before God is that it is the route to discovering God's power. The Great Litany is not the only prayer that models this movement from fault to restoration. It is seen again when confession gives way to an absolution or the assurance of forgiveness through the 'comfortable words' of scripture. Similarly, the restorative meal in which we 'give thanks' to God for Jesus work for us (the Eucharist) should always occur after the symbolic seeking and receiving forgiveness from each other in the passing of the peace. For the Christian vulnerability that comes through our faults is not fatal, but rather the route by which we may experience God's restoration.

Not all our vulnerability is caused through fault. The reality is that sooner or later we must confront our own limitation. Whether this is through illness or death, or via the many disappointments and incomplete activities which litter our lives, we learn that we are not sufficient for all things. Yet the shape of Christian worship offers great freedom in accepting our weakness. Not simply 'leaning in' to it but accepting in God's sight this aspect of our vulnerability. The modern Australian prayerbooks get this right as they place the prayers of intercession after hearing and digesting God's word. In this way, we are invited to consider the reality of our lives as compared to God's, and can then ask for sustenance despite our lack. We are set free from imprisonment to our insufficiency and given the opportunity to discover God's sustaining hand.

Blessed vulnerability

The philosopher Emanuel Levinas writes searchingly about the interplay between strength and vulnerability. For Levinas, it was the interaction between individuals that had the potential to elevate both and give them a hitherto undiscovered strength. He used the term 'face' to describe that fleeting glimpse we might have into the hidden parts of a person's being. Ironically, it was not a full gaze on the physical nose, eyes, ears and mouth that Levinas was describing, but rather something like the impression caught, as if from the 'corner of your eye', when we see a person's struggle and pain. For Levinas to 'behold the vulnerable face of the other' is to have the highest of human experiences because it cuts through our own self-absorption to the true reality of another's existence. In this sense, the vulnerability of the other was a gift not to be exploited, but to grant the opportunity to draw near in compassion.[9]

Being vulnerable is not a pleasant experience. It can often be the beginning of abuse or deprivation. There is no justification for

---

9   G. L. Bruns, *'Blanchot/Levinas: Interruption (On the Conflict of Alterities)'*, Research in Phenomenology, 26(1), p. 138.

the abuse of a vulnerable person. Levinas' words are not laying the expectation that apparent strength or capacity should be shunned or avoided. Neither are they setting up a situation in which those with power can succeed to subjugate others by appealing to their goodness. Rather these words are a plea to those of us who act as if we are sufficient on our own terms. Glorying in one's own strength quickly becomes ugly, as the capacity is used to dominate and dismiss others. Perhaps the saddest manifestation of strength, though, is self-delusion. To be confronted with failure and insufficiency, and have nowhere to turn for help, is crushing.

Glenn Morrison takes Levinas' language of 'face' further by correlating it with the vulnerability that comes from not being in charge. The mere presence of another person, particularly if that person is pushed to the margins of life, demands something from me. Yet it is not for me, initially, to be jumping to conclusions and filling up their need. To do this would mean that I am forcing myself upon them. Rather, my primary call is to draw close in compassion, or as Morrison calls it, friendship.[10] I give up my right to be right because I want to draw close to you. This is a demanding movement. It is much easier for me to order the world around me as if I were in charge. Yet this ease presumes that I have the capacity to judge what is right and furthermore put it into action.

The ultimate example of this willing self-emptying can be found in Jesus Christ. The early Christian hymn, which is found in Philippians 2, glories in Jesus' willing choice to 'let go' of what had rightfully and eternally been his, as the second member of the Trinity, for us. He emptied himself, through layers of humiliation, until nothing more could be stripped away. However, the hymn does not end at this lowest point, because Jesus' experience did not end there either. Having

---

10 G. Morrison, *Living at the Margins of Life: Encountering the Other and Doing Theology*, Australian EJournal of Theology, Feb 2006(6).

willingly let go, Jesus experienced the progressive restoration of what had been foregone. Yet the restoration did not occur through a further act of his will or might. Rather it was through the working of the other persons of the Trinity. God the Father stepped in through the Spirit to raise Jesus up. He was empty no longer, and the risk he took in beholding our vulnerability was not in vain.

Jesus saw our need, and acted out of his own, willing vulnerability. He was both the one who acted with compassion, and the one who received the benefit of God's compassionate hand. Jesus' choice to let go of what he was due, so that we might have life, forms the template and enabling heart of our own existence. In Jesus, we have both the example of how a vulnerable life may be sustained in God's plan, and the constitutional demand that any strength we have to offer is only a strength made active by God in-and-through our weakness.

Ministry is like holding an egg...

One of the difficult aspects of church life for us to get right, is to behave with each other corporately in the same way that we individually gain life. We can often extend generosity, understanding and forgiveness between ourselves as individuals. One on one, we can be gracious with each other's vulnerability. It is much more difficult to apply this same grace in embracing vulnerability in our corporate life. What we love about being Christian as individuals, and practise one on one, can be forgotten when we make decisions as a whole. Our anxieties about the future of the organisation, whether it be locally as congregations or over larger areas, can override our sense of dependence on God's sufficiency in the face of our insufficiency.

The tension between anxiety and blessed vulnerability means that our ministry for, with and from each other is like holding an egg. If, driven by anxiety, we try to grasp too hard, it will break. If we are careless, it will fall. The trick is to hold our ministry well, without falling for decisions that do not honour the need for God's sustaining hand. Four thoughts have helped me to trust in God's sustenance, while remaining diligent in ministry.

Thought 1: God never promises power or position. The story of the early church was one of powerlessness and scant authority. Similarly, the church is strongest today in places under pressure and without outward strength. God does promise comfort in distress and sustenance in-and-through difficult times. The expression of church is linked to, but not coterminal with, the spiritual reality of church. The glory we share with Jesus is, for the moment, largely hidden. It will eventually be seen. However, in either case, it is the people who, like branches grafted into the vine, are glorious. The structures that must be there to express our shared life will only reflect the hidden reality imperfectly. They will always, and must always, change to meet realities of the moment, even though they be in-and-through difficulty.

Thought 2: Much of our anxiety, surrounding the future of Christianity and the church, is driven by the structures that hold it. God continues to change people, and people continue to find life in God. In the Western world, our holding-structures do seem to creak and groan. Finances seem thin and espoused adherents may have dropped from previous decades. But the Christian faith continues to be passed on. We need to be flexible enough to allow the structures that hold the church to be adapted or die without thinking that the church has failed. For this, eyes that see the work God is doing need to be freed from being locked into where our organisations groan.

Thought 3: Mission is not meant to prop-up or sustain a structure. Rather, mission is an expression of our being companions with God on God's endeavour. The continuing expression of an organisation in any one place is a happy by-product of mission, but it is not the mission itself. To have people contentedly dependent upon God's sustaining power in-and-through their vulnerability is the heart of being engaged with God. Inevitably, this dependence will invite others to join, it will confront errant and unjust activities, it will care for the earth and those who are weak, it will even result in church organisations growing. However, these are the marks or fruit of the mission. The structures which enable churches or support and hold the mission, are a step further back, they are not the mission itself.

Thought 4: So, love God, love each other, love the world around you...and see what happens. Easy to say, but much harder to do! You may remember that Pam, the creator of such wonderful morning teas, ruled the kitchen as a tyrant. The sad reality is that those who did not venture into the kitchen enjoyed the opportunity that the refreshments provided, but those who sought to help were quickly burned by Pam's demanding presence. A beautiful, willing expression of love for God's people had turned on itself, becoming a forced act of the will, losing its connection to the God who inspired it in the first place. I wonder what would happen if Pam stepped back and found a way to serve out of her weariness. What other expressions could grow?

Here are three questions to ask
as we do not try too hard!

1

Where do I find restoration and freedom in-and-through vulnerability? How is this an expression of God's provision?

2

What are the primary factors behind the decisions I make when engaging in ministry? What are the driving factors for my congregation?

3

Where have I (we) allowed anxiety for the maintenance of the outward expression of the church to override a willing dependence on God's sustaining hand? Where might this be different?

Part B

Ten reasons to be hopeful

REASON ONE

*God is the God of the upside-down kingdom.
How exciting!*

There is no shortage of ways to be disheartened as we think about the church. Especially when we consider the church in western lands. It seems that wherever we look there is a chronicle of the decline of Christianity. Commentators either bemoan or celebrate empty churches, but they do agree that the churches seem empty. Ground is lost, and it is difficult to imagine how it could be recovered.

It is worth asking what ground is perceived as lost, before we think more deeply about this disheartening feeling. The commentary and discussions, which promote a feeling of loss or emptiness, usually focus on four points. The first: numbers of people attending church. A hard look at the data shows that while the people in church in Australia, as a percentage of the overall population, has declined, the basic number has remained steady, certainly for the last 30 years. While we may wish more would join us, it is not quite the same as saying that the church is losing people. The second: (related to the first) acute awareness of the financial pressure associated with building maintenance and ministers' salaries. While we may wish this were not so, trawling through the minutes of meetings from past years shows that the same concerns have always been with us. Third: the sale of church buildings. This may seem regrettable, but in actual fact, the buildings required to service the body of Christ is linked more to demographic spread and speed of transportation than numbers of people. That is, as people move around, less buildings are needed in some areas, and more in others. Fourthly: 'missing generations' in the pews. It seems that some generations do not relate to church life as they once did. Of all the reasons to be disheartened I think this is the greatest. Yet our upside-down God gives us cause to be hopeful.

A final reason, which may drive our sense of losing ground, is the growing perception that the Church at large no longer has a significant place within the heart of western public life. Rarely are Christian leaders, let alone representatives of any church, asked for comment on social or political matters. Further, many of those who do lead or make comment, forcefully deny the right to a Christian opinion in public affairs. This is a clear reminder that as a church we have lost the respect of many, and declining influence has followed. To be honest, this really should not surprise us. Having lived through the awful revelations of the Royal Commission into Institutional Responses to Child Sexual Abuse, we can understand there are many aspects of church life that undermine our moral authority. However, it is not simply respect and influence that have changed, these speak to our lost power and prestige.

So where is the encouragement and cause for hope? It lays in the character of God, who is the God of an upside-down kingdom. Throughout scripture we can see that God has a heart for those who are weak and downtrodden. This transcends a mere preference for weakness against strength: it is a settled desire to see those who are set aside in this world rise in God's kingdom. The usual way of the world is that the strong, wealthy, clever and well connected prevail. The consistent story of scripture is that the powerful are brought low, and the weak and surprising are lifted up. Indeed, this can be found in the Babel events, which bracket the Bible. The attempt to build the Tower of Babel (Genesis 11) can be read as an exertion of human power and control over dependence on God. The consequence is a clear dispersal of the strong, who wished to build their own name. The final two chapters of Revelation see this dispersal reversed as the many different types of people (and their languages) are brought into a city God has made. The effects of self-exertion are rolled back as the riches of the earth add to the beauty of God's land. In-between the two brackets we see God giving grace and strength to those who lay their weakness before him, and those who seek to make a name for themselves consistently denied.

In this sense, the kingdom that God is intent on bringing is an upside-down kingdom. It does not conform to the usual pattern where the strong rise and then dominate the weak. Rather, the one who is strong provides the ready foundation upon which *all* may build. It also means that each of us who build on this foundation are recruited and enabled by God to lift up those who possess only slight strength. Finally, it forces us to accept the assistance of those whom God has provided to give us aid.

In many ways, we have, as a body of western Christians, become accustomed to acting as the strong amongst the world. We have too easily fallen for the illusion that we have a name that must be exerted. So, losing apparent power and prestige is a helpful and healthful correction. If the heart of our worry is that we can no longer command respect, then it is to our benefit that we should be forced back on God's enabling hand. Losing power and prestige – how exciting!

So, the task is to discover new ways to live in God's upside-down kingdom: where we are not self-sufficient but dwell with the surprising sustenance that comes from a God determined to lift up those who build on him. The answers are not always easy, either to digest or implement. But they are good.

And the missing generations? In the west, a curious thing has occurred. The many, who make up the cohort of missing ones, actually find the Christians they know to be kind, loving and praiseworthy people. We Christians are usually attractive when taken one by one. It is the whole lot of us, when acting as a group, that can be hard to stomach. I wonder what would happen if our corporate life reflected more closely the things that are attractive about our personal faith?

REASON TWO

Jesus' body still has not been produced

Some questions are quite natural. In a sense they are obvious. We have planned hard for a holiday and the special event is on the horizon. We begin to wonder: How will we get there? Who will drive? What clothes will we need? (And if one has teenagers) Do we really need to comb our hair?

The strange thing is that the more familiar we are with the answer, the less likely we are to even ask the most obvious of questions. Easter time provides us with a ready example. Who is buying the eggs for the Easter Egg hunt? The question does not even get asked because, of course, Mum will!

We start the Easter story with a very natural question, which our familiarity causes us to dismiss, 'Who will roll away the stone?' (Mark 16:3). If we pause at this point, rather than rushing on to the rest of the story, we discover some important things that meet and nourish us even 2000 years later.

Three women, Mary, Mary and Salome, were the first to ask the question. It was a very natural question for them to ask. Jesus had just been killed by the Roman legionaries, the masters of execution. He had been buried in an ordinary tomb that had been turned into the equivalent of a high-security military installation. The women themselves were vulnerable and acting with incredible bravery amid great fear. What is more, they asked the question while coming to grips with the finality of the circumstances. One could not get more dead than this. Jesus was finished, and their hopes and dreams had died with him. This trip to the tomb was to be a final act of devotion before surrendering to hopelessness.

The benefit to us in slowing down and asking the question, 'Who will roll away the stone?' along with Mary, Mary and Salome, is that we can begin to resonate with their experience. Any one of us who has felt frightened, small, overwhelmed, insecure and hopeless has had cause to ask, 'Who will intervene in this hopeless task for me?'. Mary, Mary and Salome may have had a different task or role, but it is the same question.

Having asked the question, Mary, Mary and Salome were confronted with an odd occurrence (verse 4). The stone had already been rolled away! Their thoughts were not of resurrection. We see this by the alarm they felt. The displaced stone alluded to desecration and the malicious use of power. Had those who killed Jesus needed to do evil on his yet dead body? What more could be demanded of them! And making things even more alarming, the women were confronted by an odd young man. Clothed in white, and entirely unexpected. Clearly an angel. The insertion of the divine into the narrative enhances their distress.

But let us ponder this angel. Unlike the demi-god and superhero-characters of modern fiction, biblical angels are bearers of news. They are messengers just as their name implies (*angelos* (GK), literally means 'messenger'). This odd being was to bring a message of a stunning new reality.

Against all hope, the stone that had been rolled away had not been moved through malicious intent. Against all fear, the stone that had been rolled away did not pile desecration upon destruction. Rather, Jesus has been raised (verse 6). And with these simple words the angel brought comfort, compassion and a new fact to weave into their story.

Mary, Mary and Salome's alarm was understandable, but the first move of this messenger is to comfort, 'do not be alarmed'. In their brave yet frightened state this news was to bring calm and peace. But comfort without compassion is cold comfort. The angel understands the source of their distress. They were looking for Jesus. They wanted to do one last thing for him before it was all over. They were acting out of love even as everything came tumbling down. They were seen and recognised. They mattered. But this was not the end. There was some new information for them to process. Jesus' body was no longer there, 'see, there is the place where he (used to) lay'.

I find it interesting how the story unfolds. If God is powerful enough to bring Jesus back to life from the dead then it is entirely within reason that Jesus should return with overwhelming force, dominating all things and riding over everyone. But he creeps in. Through the messenger, God is meeting Mary, Mary and Salome quietly in their need. God introduces that part of this stunning new reality: God is intent on meeting our need rather than simply rolling over our lack.

This is where Mary, Mary and Salome's unique task and our lives intertwine. Jesus' death and resurrection open up for us the possibility of help outside of ourselves. Jesus' sacrificial, representative death, and its unfettered acceptance by God, gives unsought, lifechanging fulfilment of that most natural question, 'who will intervene in this hopeless task for me?'.

The easiest way to kill this hope, and the uncomfortable consequences it has for human power structures that wish to dominate and control, is to produce a body. The body was not produced. Indeed, there is more textual evidence for its actual life than that of Julius Caesar. No wonder Mary, Mary and Salome are remembered and admired. They were among the first to hear of a stunning new reality. Jesus is risen! May we be brave, even as we fear.

REASON THREE

People keep on being changed

It is easy to become dismayed by the obvious challenges the church faces. It can be disheartening to hear the clear declarations dismissing Christianity as a relic of the past or an unhelpful aberration in the present. However, people keep being changed by their encounter with Jesus.

For me, keeping my eyes opened to the many different things God does, is one of the challenges of life. When I find myself becoming downhearted or distressed by what seems to be ignorance or dismissal of God, I am inevitably cheered when I raise my eyes from the matters in front of me and begin to look outwards. It is as if my worry or distress acts like fear, narrowing my gaze and preventing a full view of reality. When looking up from my limited view I discover wonderful ways that God keeps transforming people.

I think of one parishioner who has been cast aside in relationship and had her interests squashed. Yet in the last few years she has taken up a musical instrument and gains great joy in her growing proficiency and the opportunity to perform. She has begun a collection of instruments each with a different tone for different purposes. She has taken lessons to develop her skill and enjoys the group she plays with. However, her increased confidence had its beginning with the patient friendship of a small congregation who helped her to sing out praises to God and hear that she was loved by Jesus. And this little congregation continues to share her new joys and help her carry on through remaining disappointment.

This small story is one of many where the effect of encountering Jesus flows into practical, life-giving benefit. I know others who have found peace in bereavement, or hope instead of hopelessness, restoration from guilt, and calm in distress. The wonder of these encounters is that they have extraordinary outcomes but usually occur in such ordinary ways.

My friend's story is so common that we can easily miss it. It has at least three aspects that reflect the different ways God interacts with each person, and that we play our part. Our anxiety around the progress or status of the church can lead us to forget that in spiritual matters God remains firmly in the driving seat. It is God who calls, be it in a still small voice or a thunderclap. God is the one who is before us and behind us: all of our being is grounded in God, who draws us onto the divine being. So, in the midst of our anxiety, we must be careful to allow God to call. Being too pushy risks misplacing what God is uniquely able to do with our own endeavour. By giving us all things through Jesus, the Father has prepared all we need for any challenge of life. By sending the Spirit, the Father and Son have released the enlivening power that we cannot summon for ourselves.

One of the things I love about my friend is that she was also active in this story. She made tenacious acts of faith, even in difficult times. If we can run the risk of missing God's activity, we can do the same in failing to recognise the steps of faith that others take when God calls. These steps may well be small: certainly mine are! But they remain acts of faith. As God calls, the Spirit's activity is met by our will. The delight of faith is that even a wavering will is enlivened and brought God-ward by the Spirit's work. Our small response is met and enlarged by God. The hesitant act of trust is met (and in old-fashioned language) proved worthwhile as God's Spirit confirms the fitness of the response. God is shown to be faithful.

Yet, we are not without our role. We are not simply an audience in a heavenly theatre, or bystanders on a coincidental scene. Rather, we too are actors in a divine drama. This restrains our over-bold and forward hand, while simultaneously ennobling our activity and endowing us with great purpose. Our role is to draw alongside each other, whether as members of Christ's body or with those who are yet to be incorporated, to nurture and encourage each other's capacity to heed God's call. In this sense we are like spiritual archaeologists who delight in discovering what God has laid down in the lives of others so that they can take hold of their own heritage. I imagine the patient task of a friend helping to brush away the sandy accretions of my existence so that the foundations of a God-ward life are recognised. You cannot change me, you should not force me, but I hope you will remind me of God's intentions for the world and help me to discover how I find my place in it.

This three-way drama is rarely loud. It usually takes a long time. We are often only aware of small parts of the whole story. But it does happen, each and every day, despite what may be said.

REASON FOUR

The seeming contraction of Christianity in the west and north of the world, balanced by huge growth in the east and south – often despite powerlessness

We are very aware of our own context. Those who are older remember times when services were more frequent, and the pews were fuller. Even those who are younger feel the sense of being part of a minority, certainly if they regard regular church attendance as important. Unlike days gone by, church leaders have little influence in society: they are more likely to be caricatured or ignored. It is easy for us to become discouraged by this, which in turn can tend to make us short-sighted. Our story seems to be the only story.

Being an Anglican, I love the question, 'Whom do you think is the average Anglican?'. Our experience and perspective will probably lead us to think of an older, white person. Probably retired, and likely to have grandchildren. The reality is quite different! The average Anglican is black, about 30 years old, has a number of her own children in tow, and is probably a member of Mother Union. For me, this beautifully illustrates a grand story that we miss if our eyes are fixed on our story alone.

The last thousand years may be viewed as a 'European' millennium. The exploits and expansion of European peoples have had a global influence. While the value and rightness of many aspects of this expansion can and should be questioned, the legacy of Christianity is deeply woven into Europe and the places where European people settled. Yet these last decades have written a new story with new Christian heartlands. Whether Anglican, Roman Catholic, an Orthodox expression, or one of the evangelical or Pentecostal free churches, the weight of numbers now sits in Asia and Africa; the east and south. What is even more exciting than the simple example that churches can and are being filled elsewhere, is that we are living in a time in which leadership in the church is transferring from the world's north and west to the east and south.

When we think of leadership, it is often the people in obvious and titled roles whom we imagine. It is certainly true that the east and south have capable and inspiring leaders in formal roles. However, it is the generalised leadership that excites me. The sort that comes as people with a range of backgrounds, and the inevitable broadening of perspective, have their voices come to the fore. Listening to people, whom we are not used to hearing speak of Jesus, raise their voices in worship in their own language and wrestle over scripture, can help us – accustomed as we are to think of ourselves as being at the centre of world Christianity – to learn and grow. Our blind spots, conundrums and comfortable transgressions can be exposed and dealt with, as others from a different starting point unsettle our ease.

Much of the growth that has occurred in the east and south has had a long genesis. In some ways, we in the west are only waking up to what has actually been growing for years. Yet, new growth is also occurring. Much as the churches pioneered by the Ethiopian court official in the Book of Acts, or St Patrick, who both returned to their homelands to share the great news of Jesus, new churches are being planted in lands that have not had an indigenous Christianity. An example of this in the Anglican world, comes from Nepal. At great personal cost, a small team of newly-ordained Nepalese clergy are pastoring a chain of small congregations throughout the mountainous land. Poverty, scant resources and opposition from those with a vested interest in the status quo, have not prevented this new work. Furthermore, they have been equipped and sent not by Europeans, but by Asians.

The common thread in the growing churches in the east and south is an earthly powerlessness. It would be wrong to romanticise poverty or spiritualise the value of being prevented freedom. These often accompany powerlessness. However, for those of us used to having great autonomy and privilege, the realisation that the centre of our faith is found amongst those without these advantages should give us cause for thought. Is the freedom we enjoy and the resource we hold essential to a thriving church? Are the comforts that come with self-determination helpful to deep faith and a flourishing spiritual life?

The gift that others bring to us is not confined to what is given to us. While I think that we have much more to receive from the new heartlands than to give, we do have the opportunity to share. One of the great acts of God is to restore a disunited and fractured humanity. To have opportunity to relate to a growing and vibrant church, which is culturally different from our own, is a tangible expression of God's Kingdom. It is an element of the kingdom being here on earth as it is in heaven. We have the chance to engage in open and generous fellowship with these parts of God's church. It is likely to have its prickly and disappointing moments as our differences confront each other. However, I suspect that the more difficult the interaction, the greater the blessing each party will receive, as each will become more like the people God is redeeming as his own.

REASON FIVE

Still the best language for significant moments in life!

Historically, the church in Australia has played a considerable role in social observances. This may have been through the liturgical recognition of significant life events such as births, marriages and deaths. It may have been through the organisation and coordination of community social gatherings, including social sports clubs and dances. Many of these activities, such as the social sporting leagues, have ceased and only a few remain. The general community infrastructure now provides an outlet for many of the social pastimes the church once fulfilled. It stands to reason that when people no longer see the church as a community hub, then the organised activities it provides will fall away and other entities fill the need.

It seems that the liturgical set pieces, which mark the milestones of life, have also become less important for many. The observance of births, significant relationships and death have all become less likely to occur in churches. The Christian acts of baptism, marriage and the funeral seem to occur less frequently than in even the recent past, as people choose other ways of marking the significant occasion. I suspect this is because the idea of attending a church to commemorate these life events seems odd. However, the alternatives being sought provide little more than a lavish party. This leads me to wonder whether baptism, the wedding and funeral can, counterintuitively, grow in their significance.

The reason I am optimistic, and we have cause for hope, is the significant difference between what is commonly expressed as commemorations for key events and the spiritual import of baptism and a Christian wedding and funeral. Wanting to mark key stages in life is as unsurprising as it is common. However, each Christian liturgical act, which has accompanied these significant occasions, is not simply an archaic way of saying that something special has happened. Rather the liturgical acts provide a specifically crafted language for people to bring these major events to God. So, while a baptism, wedding or funeral had been associated with a broad range of general social activities to commemorate births, marriages and deaths, they were not simply one and the same with the social observance. At its best the party held after a baptism brought a community together to enjoy the beginning of a new life even as they prayed for the child's growing faith. Yet the party was not the same as the baptism. This applies for weddings and funerals too.

Each of the occasions prompting a baptism, a wedding or a funeral open a small window to eternity that a simple party cannot adequately address. The birth of a child brings the realisation of extraordinary beauty and promise while attended by weariness and stress. The movement of a relationship to the point of commitment for life sees the paradox of growth and depth even as the relationship is defined and restricted. The death of a loved one, or even one who was significant but not loved, creates a range of conflicting emotions that wash over our very sense of being.

A party is inadequate to address these forces, and secularised observances are not much better. As inheritors of the Christian story, we have the extraordinary blessing of words and ways to capture the beauty, pain and challenge of each of these momentous events even as we do so before God. The poverty of the common secular approaches will only become more obvious and unsatisfying. This does not mean that people will necessarily make their own way to the church to find the richness of what we have to offer. Rather it is likely they will not. However, we have a host of new opportunities now that a generalised and low-level party has been detached from the spiritual benefit we have to offer.

For us to take up these opportunities we need to be sensitive to the changed social position we occupy. We are not the hub of a social network, but instead have the chance to be servants, teaching a spiritually poor community the language they lack. As such, our challenge is to pivot from set pieces to openings for God-ward relationship. To expect people to come and gain from what we know to be deep and satisfying, assumes that they already value our activity. Ironically, this turns a baptism, wedding or funeral into a product to be accessed or discarded. There are three flow-on effects of this attitude for the church: a self-defeating laziness; frustration as the few who come treat our offering as a product to be consumed and the husk discarded; a failure to grasp the opportunity to serve well.

There is great cause for hope though if we take hold of opportunities to draw alongside those in our communities who are experiencing a window to eternity, but do not have the language to describe, let alone respond well, to it. The liturgical set pieces can and should be the high point of this engagement, but the role of patient conversation and preparation of people is enhanced greatly. Patient conversation rests on two prior aspects; knowledge and a bit of courage. To be able to converse well, especially about important things, requires us to know our conversation partner well. This is the sort of self-giving knowledge that does not look to simply tick off a series of key facts, but exhibits a deep curiosity about how the other person lives and feels. It is self-giving when our curiosity is sparked by a desire to value the other and be concerned for their well-being. Conversation begins with listening, but it is a shared experience. Many who perceive a window on eternity, but are bewildered by the experience, will value the opportunity to hear our take on what it signifies and how to move past a vague recognition in order to discover the God who dwells there. We have this knowledge and, with a bit of courage, can gently share what we know.

REASON SIX

We are the only ones who can truly claim a national presence

Civic and commercial institutions have been withdrawing from small communities for many years now. Even larger towns are finding that the services and businesses they once hosted are shutting up shop. Government entities are now universally centralised in the metropolises and a handful of regional centres. The shop-front service hubs are also being located in large towns, with the expectation that access will be primarily through the phone or internet. Banks, mechanics, service stations and even supermarkets can no longer keep their doors open, and are withdrawing from smaller communities. This shrinkage to the centre is felt acutely in the rural and regional parts of Australia (having always been this way in the remote areas), but it is not felt by country Australians alone. As our large cities get even bigger, there are entire regions within the cities that have lost their local services.

I am not necessarily being critical of those who have had to close and move. The demands arising in trying to serve a vast and sparsely populated land are immense. In some ways, the rise of sophisticated communications technology has been a boon for a land such as ours. Aspects of daily life have been made easier and more efficient through the use of information and communications technology. Similarly, the move to centralise specialised services in high-density areas makes economic sense. The costly and collaborative nature of these skilled activities does tend to drive the development of centralised, specialised hubs. However, these understandable moves have consequences for us all. Whether it is the drive for disembodied and depersonalised digital transactions, or the removal of people with key skills from locally accessible communities, we lose out on face-to-face relational engagement with people who can help us.

In a world where services are reduced to transactions, and relationships with people are downplayed, claims for national coverage are easy to make. As long as any of us has a mobile phone, a government or corporation can claim to reach everywhere. But those who have been frustrated by the inability to work-through a question via a website or call centre, or have been forced to travel for many hours or days to access relatively routine health or dietary needs, know that these claims are somewhat hollow.

So, who else can claim a truly national coverage? Churches – the many little ones dotted throughout the suburbs, towns, villages and hamlets of Australia! The congregations that still meet in large and small places throughout the land belie the well-known decline of Christianity as the nationally espoused spirituality. At its heart, Christianity is about people, and people meeting together. It cannot be reduced to a series of transactions or downloadable order forms. As people hold the Christian faith, their urge is to meet – so they do.

It is true that church buildings need to be sold, and some congregations do fold. However, there is another story that exists beneath the one that often makes the headline. It is rare that Christian people, who have faced the sad reality of their small congregation deciding to stop meeting, actually cease meeting themselves. Usually, they will seek out and find hospitable inclusion with another congregation in their locality. Sometimes, this will result in whole-hearted immersion in the new denomination, other times it may be more like a cousin being cared for in a new home. Either way denominational adherence becomes less important than continuing Christian fellowship.

This is exciting for two reasons. It is tangible evidence of Jesus' promise to protect his church (Matt 16:17–19). It could well be argued that, by being forced to collaborate, Christians are being given the opportunity to show visibly what the universal, Catholic church is, spiritually. This benefit has great value for us who make up the church. But there is a missional benefit as well. The same people who populate the little congregations dotted throughout Australia also tend to be the ones who are active in their communities. They are frequently the ones who provide care and help to the community in times of need. The same passion and energy they put into preserving a life of corporate worship will often be poured into the other groups that make community life safe and fulfilling. The few remaining local community hubs, such as sporting clubs, volunteer emergency services and welfare groups, will often be served by the same Christians who pull the congregation together.

By preserving the relationships that nurture and encourage social cohesion, Christian people are very often loved and valued by their communities. The heart that prioritises relationship over expedience is winsome and difficult not to appreciate. However, even while loving the Christians individually and valuing their work to help local districts tick, many who are not Christian have simply forgotten that these same people are the church! The bank has gone, Centrelink is inaccessible and the telcos mystifying, but the church is there because Pal and Pam are.

I experienced this firsthand during one of my pastoral charges. There was one protestant congregation in town and one Roman Catholic, and I was the only resident minister. This meant that the small, faithful congregation I served tended not to think of themselves as Anglican. We were a very mixed bag. Our building was on a large bush block in the literal centre of town. However, locals would often ask me where it was. As the scrub had grown and obscured the church building, they had forgotten. Yet, whenever there was need in town, or someone fell on hard times, the three people who were inevitably sought out were keen and core members of the congregation. The community knew intuitively they would find compassion and help. One year I invited the local volunteer fire brigade to use the church block as the site for their practise burns. Once the bush was tamed it was amazing how many people exclaimed in surprise that the church was so close. The next challenge was reminding them that the people who loved and cared for them were even closer.

REASON SEVEN

Connectedness is in our DNA

Christians are connected. Uniting a fractured world is one of the fruits of God's activity. Jesus came so that the differences that exist between people of all types would no longer be cause for division (Gal 3:28). This does not mean that a sort of bland uniformity will be imposed, but rather a harmonious enjoyment of the variety that God has built into the world. This is illustrated beautifully in the closing verses of Revelation when the 'kings and queens of the world' stream into God's fulfilled Kingdom bringing the richness of their peoples in too (Rev 21:24). I take this to be a deep reflection on the enjoyment that is released as a united, redeemed humanity are able to live out the freedom of relationship that God has made possible.

However one views the connection between the picture presented in Revelation and our present-day experience, we are called by God to be drawn to each other, whether we like it or not. By being connected to God through Jesus Christ, we are also connected to all those others who are similarly bound to Jesus. This has both local and global aspects.

Locally, we see our connectedness play-out through the weekly life of congregations. The many small activities showing this connection abound: phone calls to check up on each other's wellbeing; food hampers and meals delivered to those who are sick; lifts taking the housebound to medical appointments. The larger gatherings to share in prayer, praise and nurture along with the regular small-group meetings are quite unusual when compared to the somewhat restrained and limited relational lives many people lead.

Globally, this is expressed through the weekly intercessory prayers in which we should be bringing the needs of others before God. For this to occur, we have cultivated an interest in the welfare and daily life of others. This is particularly acute in a concern for the care of the dispossessed and vulnerable. Before we get too impressed by this other-person-centred approach it is only true because it is a reflection of God's own heart. When we cease to pray for others and be broken by their wounds, we are on a slippery slope away from faith in Christ. However, when compassion reigns it cannot help but ask questions of our daily life, and prompt more ethical approaches to living, because the impact of our activities on those in need are more likely to be known.

As an educated, comfortable white male, I can remember catching my first conscious glimpse of the horrible effects of dispossession and poverty. It was through a Brazilian heavy metal band. I had bought a cassette containing a song about life in the favelas of Belo Horizonte (the unmistakably entitled *Dead Embryonic Cells*) and the cover showed a picture of the band sat in the streets amidst an overcrowded and depressed neighbourhood. It cut through my comfort, and in time helped to open my eyes to some of what I had missed closer to home. However, this realisation began to change my behaviour through a garden-variety endeavour of the church. Having been moved, I wanted to be engaged in something through which I might share out of my wealth. The opportunity to join a mission organisation focussed on South America provided the way for me to take my growing understanding further, being engaged with actual people in South America and not simply an idea. This link has endured, and I remain connected, in various ways, to that continent.

I suspect that the manner in which we have our eyes opened to the needs and blessings of others will not always occur in the same way. Indeed, probably not many will have shared my particular epiphany! However, the next step is very common as the interconnectedness of the church provides practical ways for us to live out something bigger and more fulfilling than our own interests. The various personal friendships and organisations that abound, because of the essential unity of the church, provide an unusually deep and extensive network when compared to many of those with whom we rub shoulders. Regular opportunities to enable community development projects to go ahead in other places, prayer notes, and mission spots in church all contribute to specific and reliable knowledge about life for real people in other areas. Personal friendships with those who live and serve as missionaries in different nations provide a bridge to relationship with real people in those lands. The ordinary Christian infrastructure of relationship gives us access to each other in a way that those who are not part of the church do not have.

The ordinary activities of the church promote practical, unfussy ways to make a difference to people, be they near or far. This is because to be part of the church means being bound to all those others who are similarly united to Christ. It is part of our DNA. However, the desire to relate to people well, to share their beauty, and to help fill their need is not unique to the church. Many people without a Christian faith also want the sort of deep connection that is taken for granted in church life. Indeed a sense of local and global connection that has practical outcomes is an espoused value of the broad community. Yet, I do wonder whether there are the mechanisms, to put this value into action, that we take for granted.

One way we as the church can serve a community that desires local and global connection is to make our everyday activities, which nurture connection, visible and accessible. Connection is part of our

DNA. Biologically, DNA has the incredible capacity to replicate; to share its nature. I wonder whether the gift of being together, with which God has endowed us, can be replicated as we share our nature.

REASON EIGHT

We have 'franchises' everywhere

Our generation has witnessed the rise of the large, coordinated business. Fast food outlets, hardware stores and service stations are now almost uniformly part of a franchise. Even the usually localised approach to landscaping and garden maintenance has jumped on to the trend. There is much to dislike and dismiss about this tendency. The friendly neighbourhood shop, which could stock a range of brands and be staffed by passionate locals, seems to be a thing of the past. However, the broad spread of products and services of a uniform quality is something we now take for granted. It is hard to imagine rolling in to one of the large service stations only to find that the bowsers are empty. Even in the bush!

Although the rise of the franchise has not been entirely without its downsides, at its best it enables the distribution of resources and energy in a coordinated manner. In many ways the Christian church does this, and even makes up for some of the pitfalls of franchised businesses. Irrespective of denomination, the inescapable localism of the church spreads outposts of faith throughout the land. It would be much easier for each denomination to centralise their congregations into single massive units. It would be a much more efficient way to run. The overheads associated with buildings would be lessened, the numbers of clergy and other ministry workers minimised, and the streaming and specialisation of services would be enhanced. Yet, of course, this will not happen! Centralising into a handful of megachurches reduces each person's engagement with God, their access to relational pastoral care and nurture, and their ability to be involved in ministry. It cuts against the relational heart of Christianity. The church is inescapably local. It must be.

So, strangely enough, the distribution of congregations worshipping God throughout Australia would be the envy of the most aggressive of franchising businesses. We have franchises everywhere. Unlike large hardware businesses, fuel selling operations or even medical centres, the many congregations scattered throughout Australia are focussed on the quality of the relationships that they enable. They are personally invested in their vertical relationship with God, as it is expressed in worship. They also yearn for good and growing horizontal relationships with their family, friends, neighbours and workmates as they bear witness to God's great work through Jesus. The potential to 'distribute' faith is unrivalled because the inescapable localism of the church is matched by their inescapable relationality.

At their best, denominations can be the drivers that enable the distribution of congregations and help to shoulder some of the organisational load, which locally and relationally oriented congregations may struggle to sustain. Not many of us look at denominational structures through rose-coloured glasses, even those of us who are intimately involved with them. However, they do fulfil at least two helpful functions. The first is to provide the sort of oversight that allows the intensely local congregations to stay on track with each other. This is not primarily coordination of key activities, indeed there should be much local discretion here. Rather, it is reminding each of us that our patch of the world, and our way of looking at Christianity, are not sufficient. They are a small reminder and spur of the church which is Catholic: universal through space and time. The second is to help take up those activities that are necessary for the function of a community within our context, but not the primary call of each Christian and their congregation. I suspect that many will think their own way of doing administration or adhering to the laws of the land may be better than their denominational way. However, I do know that the primary purpose of the congregation is to worship God well and show and tell others what a life lived in the light of Jesus is. This call should trump even our best ways of filling out forms, if there is someone else offering to do it.

The incredible distribution of God's work across Australia is not surprising. However, the fact that congregations do not typically retreat into their own, solo mode is astounding. This seeming paradox is an artefact of the same promise given by Jesus when he said that 'when two or three are gathered in my name I am with them' (Matt 18:20). The passage within which the promise is embedded deals with the difficult parts of community life, the disagreements and even hurt caused by others. The promise is for the local congregation – small and fractious as it may be. Jesus is with them as they seek to live out a God-ward life. The promise also applies when meeting with Christians who are not part of the usual community. Jesus is with this meeting too. To be spread out, embedded in our communities, is natural. To be drawn to others we do not usually see brings wonderful possibilities for encouragement and yes, even correction.

Being a person whose time is focussed on denominational things, one of my great joys is visiting and being enfolded in many congregations. In some ways, part of my job is to reassure each small congregation that they are not alone, but many are with them. It is wonderfully affirming to be taken into other peoples' hearts and is a great privilege. However, this rather personal blessing inevitably gives way to a deeper and more wonderful thing. As I am taken into these different congregations, I see their unique gifts being used to serve others and bring glory to God. They are evidence of God at work in the different towns and villages of the land. They are a tangible result of God's Kingdom coming 'on earth as it is in heaven'.

Unlike a business franchise, the congregations of the church in Australia are not uniform. Yet, they provide a deep and wide insight, for the many who are not disciples of Jesus, as to what this means. They provide a network, without parallel, of people praying, celebrating the Lord's Supper, baptising ever-new people into a new life, and listening hard for God's voice as they read his word. Even the AFL and Rugby League cannot organise this sort of association!

REASON NINE

*Those who have stayed
are highly engaged – they have to be!*

There is a surprising complement to the relative decrease in the number of people who come to church in Australia. If the declining proportion of Australians who attend church tells us that there is not the same mass adherence to Christianity than there once was, the presence of those who choose to come tells us something wonderful – they are highly engaged. To decide to come to church requires an act of the will that may not have been present in the past where other social benefits and prompts were stronger.

Like many things in our contemporary world there is a slightly complex story behind this engagement. Those who choose to come to church and regard themselves as being regular attendees do not always come every week. Indeed, the regular survey of Australian churches (the National Church Life Survey) now regards regular attendance as monthly. However, there are two aspects to this which we should note. The first is that we are talking about people who add a key activity to what they believe. That is, the beliefs which they espouse gain some practical traction in their lives as they choose to gather as part of a congregation. The second aspect is the reciprocal side of this activity. Even though the frequency of church attendance may be lower than in the past, adherence survives. Acknowledging the risks to devotion that this presents, I tend to think it shows a sense of faith that is committed despite other demands.

This committed faith is amplified when we consider some of the supporting structures, which provided a scaffold around church attendance in previous eras. The social activities and interest groups which were once run by churches have all but disappeared. The structured youth and children's programs, which had an element of catechesis but were largely socialising forces, are not universal as they once were. The hands-on social services provided at the local level by congregations are now largely assumed by professionalised agencies. Generally, the activity of a local congregation is restricted to activities of worship, the nurture of faith, and low-key acts of service. When considering those who choose to remain actively engaged in church, we should recognise that these socialising activities no longer play a role in keeping them there.

This is amplified further when we consider the discrediting role of scandals such as those posed by abuse. We have lived through a time when shameful deeds done in the name and under the cover of the church have come to light. We will continue to live with the legacy of the damage which has been done to many people by those who used Christianity to further their own diabolical aims. It is good and right that we as the church grieve over this and seek to make amends. However, even as we do so, we live within a broad community that looks with varying degrees of distrust upon the church.

It is worth us pondering what is there to come for? It is not a stretch to think that those who choose to remain engaged do so because of overriding spiritual values. I would think that there is not much else to motivate continuing commitment. Connection with each other as we connect with God would be the overwhelming reason to remain engaged. For those who have chosen to stay it is about the faith!

Some of the stresses of contemporary church life are manifestations of this high engagement. Conflicting opinions on how worship should be done; concern for where money should be spent, and stress over small budgets; contention around what decisions are made, and how they are made, are all manifestations of care. We tend not to argue if we have no abiding interest in the matter at hand. Yet, we do argue and this shows that we care.

This all adds up to my conviction that we have an engaged and committed mob. Why else in this environment would people choose to come? While it does not necessarily make planning in difficult times easier, it is important for us to pause and give God thanks for committed faith. Spiritual malaise can be masked by congregations, activities and denominations that seem to power along. To be trimmed to a committed core does not automatically make for health, but it can be the beginning of growth when the commitment is evidence of a solid foundation. To my mind this makes one disposition and one activity vital.

We should really love and be committed to those who share church with us. Even those with whom we disagree and argue. They, like we ourselves, have made significant choices to remain connected with church, and this should be a spur for us to hold them in high regard. Loving those who share church with us can often be a difficult thing, and does not mean that we aim for a sort of pleasant niceness that avoids conflict by avoiding disagreement. It does mean that when we disagree and find fault with each other we do so while remaining committed to each other. A disposition that values each other will seek to find restoration through the dispute and think carefully about how we manifest what are deeply held convictions.

A disposition that values each person who chooses to stay will then seek out ways to encourage them. If you are choosing, against many forces, to remain connected with Christ and his church, then surely my primary activity for you should be encouragement. I can do this generally, but encouragement is best when it is personal and direct. So, for me to be able to encourage you personally and directly, I need to spend time deepening my friendship with you. What are your hopes and dreams? Where do you hurt or get frustrated? Are you down of heart or full of joy? How do you best hear the words that will bolster your faith in Jesus and help you live out your call in him? I suspect I need to spend time asking you questions first!

REASON TEN

There are green shoots everywhere!

When living and working in North-West Australia I would frequently drive through the vast, dry outback. It was not uncommon to drive a thousand kilometres in a day, speeding along in an air-conditioned vehicle, insulated against the scorching heat. The distinctive red dirt reflecting the heat into ironic mirages that belied the bone-dry surface. From the car, my favourite parts seemed only to have clumps of spinifex. It was difficult to believe that anything else could survive in such a harsh environment.

Yet, when I stopped and braved the heat outside the car, another picture emerged. Speeding along in a sealed and artificially cooled bubble I had missed what was happening at my feet. When I stopped, turned off the car and braved the heat, I discovered a new world. Before I had taken many steps, a profusion of insect and small animal life was apparent, and I could see small, green shoots pushing through the dry crust. Incredible life, which I had missed, was there just waiting for me to recognise. It did not rely on me: it would be there whether I had stopped or not. But it gave me a much fuller picture of what was happening. The land I thought I knew as barren, was anything but.

This experience illustrates the reality of church life in Australia. It can feel as if we travel through a dry and inhospitable land where only the hardiest of specimens survive. Yet this is far from the truth. There are green shoots everywhere. Let me tell you about five.

The Narnia club

A small town in New South Wales had lost its Sunday School years ago. It could not keep up with the demands of teaching scripture in the local schools. Its youth group was a bare memory. But one layperson had a heart for young people…and a passion for C.S. Lewis' Narnia books. *The Lion, the Witch and the Wardrobe* had been a wonderful world for her imagination to roam and for her to see and respond to Jesus as Lewis' allegory took hold. As she shared her passion with her priest, she asked the simple question, 'Could we try a Narnia club?' And so they did. The small group of adults crafted a series of afternoon clubs where the stories from the world of Narnia opened the way for imaginative play and discussions about how Aslan represented Jesus. Guess what? A mob of children came, and came, and came again, to explore the world of Narnia too!

Supermarket worship

As the shock of the first COVID-19 lockdowns in Victoria took hold a rural parish grappled with the deep sorrow and sense of dispossession that came when church gatherings could not occur. Like many, the leaders of the parish scrambled to learn how to live-stream a basic prayer and praise service, using a smart phone and social media. The same church leaders were also dizzyingly busy seeking to provide comfort and care around their town: the grief, at being prevented from public worship, made more difficult by the weariness that comes from walking with others through their own hardship. However, this engagement with others throughout the town opened a surprising door.

The local supermarket began streaming the weekly prayer service. Live. Each Sunday. Who would have thought it!

Church without times

Another small congregation recognised that the neighbouring village did not have a Christian gathering of its own. As they prayed and watched and thought about what to do, they realised that many of the younger families who lived in the village were not accustomed to the regular schedule most of our congregations use. It conflicted with the other demands of their lives. Eventually they began the 'church without times' in the local park. It was a series of interactive stations where families could move through activities that helped them to pray, engage with scripture, and praise God through song and their creativity. The participants arrived when they could and moved around each station as they wished. After a while, the Sunday afternoon excursion to the park was planned to coincide with the chance to worship. What a day out!

Hot chips

A minister tried hard to be hospitable to the community, recognising that the church building was largely vacant during the week. So, when a few of the local lads asked whether they could use the building for their regular computer gaming activities the answer was yes. After a few months of cleaning up after the young men and setting the building back in order ready for the Sunday service, the minister thought he should try doing something to introduce a spiritual aspect to the relationship. He did not have much by way of resources or people to share the creative side of leadership, so he tried a basic plan. "Fellas, if I bought you hot chips once a week would you drop by, and I'll tell you about Jesus?" They said yes. So, they ate hot chips, read a chapter of Luke's Gospel, discussed its meaning and watched a few minutes of a video about the historicity of the Bible. And they came back week after week. The double surprise is that after the second week one of the lads quietly said, 'You don't need to buy us food, we like coming'.

Lego challenge

A children's minister put out the challenge that the best tableau or short movie made from Lego, which featured the story of Jonah, would win a small prize. Before the end of the first weekend, he had received a series of photos from a mum of pre-school children, who had raced into their room to consult their storybook Bibles and then carefully constructed scenes displaying the most important part of the story for them. Weeks later, an adult was overheard asking a different child how their stop motion movie was going. A pretty cool way to study the scriptures!

CONCLUSION

Pal, Pam, Paul the Greater and his namesake, Paul the Lesser all yearn for a thriving church where light shines and life flourishes. Like many of us, they look with envy at the things other churches do and wish that they could do them too. Similarly, they shrink before the worries and expectations of the world around them. They fear that they do not have the wisdom, strength or energy to stand up before the demands of our contemporary world.

They have discovered that there is no silver bullet or magical solution that will transform their worries and struggles into unmitigated success. For they are the very tools God has provided for the mission he has given. As much as they have sought an intervention from outside, which will fill what they lack, they have begun to realise that there are many things they can do. They will not be able to do everything, and every idea they put into practice or interaction they bravely initiate, will not bear obvious fruit. But they are the ones whom God has called to be his witnesses through St Silas by the Overpass.

> What is your call?
> Who is it that God has made you to be?
> What has God equipped you to do?
> Which part of God's mission do you fulfil?
> What step to follow Jesus is before your feet – and those of your church?

> God is enough!

www.ingramcontent.com/pod-product-compliance
Lightning Source LLC
Chambersburg PA
CBHW021440080526
44588CB00009B/611